SERVICE AND SCANDAL:

The life and times
of an immigrant Jewish clergyman

by

Daniel Appleby

ISBN: 978-0-9927967-0-9

Published by Old Montague Press, London
oldmontaguepress@gmail.com

CONTENTS

FOREWORD

This is an account of the life of David Applebaum, my grandfather, who died long before I was born. His emigration to Britain is the reason why his descendants are British and, indeed, why there are so many descendants currently living at all, given the fate of Polish Jewry. His life story is also the story of the establishment of an East End Jewish family to whom all of his descendants can trace some of their DNA, whether they are or consider themselves to be Jewish, partly Jewish or not Jewish at all.

As well-loved as he was by his family in his lifetime or fondly remembered by them afterwards, it cannot be pretended that he was a figure of immense personal achievement. Nevertheless, his story is worth telling. It is a case study of the life of an immigrant Jewish clergyman, which is revealing about Jewish society at the time. It also helps illuminate the "Circumcision Scandal" in the early years of the twentieth century, an episode in British Jewish history in which he was seriously involved and which is described here for the first time.

In his life, David Applebaum made at least four fresh starts. His mobility and adaptability, despite the weight of his domestic responsibilities, was facilitated by the functions he performed as a *chazan* (cantor), *shochet* (ritual slaughterer) and *mohel* (circumciser). The nature of these activities made it possible for him to transplant his ever larger family between distant locations and yet in each to set up home within a broadly similar Ashkenazi Jewish community where the same communal language, Yiddish, was spoken. Mobility and adaptability were helped further by the hard-won personal strengths of people who lived in a poorer and tougher time than our own. For David Applebaum and his family, resilience was a habit born of necessity.

In the late 1980s, I worked for a short period, and without any enthusiasm whatsoever, for a law firm in Holborn in London. The office was five minutes' walk from the *Jewish Chronicle*'s offices in Furnival

Street and I would escape, for as long as I could each working day, to the newspaper's library to research my grandfather's life in volumes of back editions. This was my principal source of information. No relevant personal or family papers relating to his life had survived. Nor was there anyone living among my relatives who remembered him. However, people recollected stories about him, even if they did not know when he finally settled in Britain, when he died or where he was buried. After a while, using the usual genealogical sources, interviews with family and relatives and library research, I accumulated a lot of information, which I never wrote up. It is only now (2011-3) that I have been able to go back to my material, some of it a quarter of a century old, add to it considerably, and produce a life story. The heap of facts, digressions and speculation that follows is the outcome.

1. David Applebaum Remembered

The people who provided me with hearsay information were remarkably consistent in their recollections of what they were told. I heard the same anecdotes from people who did not know each other or, if they did, had not spoken to each other for years. The picture built up was of my grandfather in the final period of his life when he was an Edwardian Jewish clergyman of modest means raising a large family in a crowded few rooms above a shop on a noisy main road in the East End of London.

The two photographs of him that survive do not convey his real personality. The earlier one (Illustration A), probably taken when he was a *chazan* in Newcastle, shows a good-looking young clergyman with a neatly-trimmed beard. In the later picture (Illustration B), taken a year or two before his death, he is a more authoritative figure, but his face bears a trace of a smile. In both pictures, he is shown to have high cheekbones and small, deep-set eyes. The photographs are formal studies that required a serious demeanour from the sitter and fail to communicate his light-hearted and easy-going nature.

He was religiously observant, but not given to extremes of piety. He was a well-loved paterfamilias and was not strict with his children. He had a wonderful tenor voice and a love of music. He was not bookish and never became very fluent in English. He had a strong sense of humour and was unashamed to tell a racy joke. He did not drink, but he liked to gamble. It was a trait all his sons inherited and for some of them it was a weakness. He might officiate at a *bris* (a Jewish ritual circumcision), but when the cards came out afterwards, as was often the case in those days, stay behind and, on at least one occasion, lose his fee. And once, so the story goes, he backed a horse without realizing until later, to his immense embarrassment, that it was to run on *Yom Kippur* (the Day of Atonement), the most solemn and holy day in the Jewish calendar. He died in circumstances that became part of family legend after a short illness at the early age of 52. There was no life insurance, although some friendly society benefits were available, and he left little to his wife and children except memories.[1]

Footnote Abbreviations:
Jewish Chronicle – *JC*
Jewish World – *JW*
Newcastle Daily Chronicle - *NDC*
London Metropolitan Archives – LMA
National Archives - NA

1   Minnie Stein recollected being told by David Applebaum's widow that when he died there was no life insurance (conversation, 21st September 1987). However, the family would have been in receipt of some friendly society benefits. David Applebaum was a member of two friendly societies in 1907, the Hebrew Order of Druids and the smaller Sons of Dobrin Benefit and Tontine Society. At the time of his death, the amount of death benefit payable to members' estates by the Hebrew Order of Druids was £25 (*JC*, 25th June 1909, p.36). The benefit payable by the Sons of Dobrin is not known, but it is unlikely to have exceeded £50.

2. Poland and Russia

David Applebaum was born in the small Polish town of Dobrzyn nad Wisla in about 1855. Poland had been an independent state in the eighteenth century, but had undergone three partitions among and between its neighbours, Russia, Prussia and Austria, finally disappearing in 1795. A semi-independent Grand Duchy of Warsaw was brought briefly into existence by Napoleon, but in 1815 this was extinguished and Poland was partitioned for a fourth time, the heartland, so-called "Congress Poland", being annexed by Russia. At first, under Russian rule, Russian Poland was permitted some autonomy and Polish continued as the official language. This period came to an end as a consequence of the unsuccessful Polish rebellion of 1830-1. Polish constitutional liberties were repealed and Poland fell entirely under Russian autocratic rule and bureaucratic government. Polish universities were closed and the use of Russian was introduced in schools. In response, Polish nationalism went underground, bursting forth again in another unsuccessful rebellion in 1861.

Within the eighteenth-century kingdom of Poland, Jews had lived everywhere, in cities, towns and villages. They provide Poland with a substantial part of its commercial class. Most Jews were not, however, prosperous bourgeois; they were petty traders, shop and tavern keepers, middlemen, contractors and craftsmen. They were despised by many elements in Polish society and denied legal rights. The disappearance of Polish independence and then, after 1831, of Polish autonomy, meant that the political fortunes of Jews in Poland were no longer solely focused on decisions taken in Warsaw. Their destiny became increasingly bound up with the fate of Jews elsewhere in the Tsar's vast dominions and with decisions taken in St Petersburg. Polish Jews now faced anti-Semitism of a cruder, harsher sort.

The reasons for the difference were historical and cultural. Jews had been encouraged to settle in Poland in the Middle Ages by Polish monarchs and noblemen who saw them as generators of wealth for the ultimate benefit of Poland's rulers. Russia now found itself with a much expanded Jewish population, which it had acquired not by immigration, but by conquest, and whose presence was not welcomed by Russia's rulers. There was long-standing anti-Semitic prejudice in Russia, fostered by the Church, and the reaction of the Tsarist authorities to the addition to the empire of large numbers of Jews was to introduce new anti-Jewish laws. The most significant of these was the establishment between 1791 and 1812 of the Pale of Settlement. This was a zone of some fifteen Russian provinces, situated on the western margins of the empire. Jews were only permitted to live in these provinces and travel elsewhere in the empire was not permitted without legal authorisation. Within the Pale, Russian authorities introduced, from 1804 onwards, a series of laws restricting where Jews might live and the occupations they might pursue. These laws were followed in 1827 by the so-called Cantonist Decrees, which rendered all Jewish males between 12 and 25 liable to military conscription, forcing younger boys into canton schools and military depots where they might be compelled to baptise into Christianity. Subsequent laws limited the publication of Jewish books, required Jewish children to attend Russian schools and forbade Jews from wearing certain items of traditional dress.

Congress Poland, the rump of the extensive pre-partition Polish state, comprised ten provinces. These were not part of the Pale; indeed, until 1862, Jews from the ten provinces of Poland were not permitted to settle in the fifteen provinces of the Pale and vice versa. As the nineteenth century progressed, the Jews of Congress Poland became increasingly subject to the same legal disabilities as the Jews of the Pale, but for many decades they benefited from less discriminatory treatment. For example, it was not until 1843 that the 1827 conscription law was extended to Congress Poland and then with several alleviations. In the words of the historian Simon Markovich Dubnow: "taken as whole, the lot of Polish Jews, sad though it was, might be pronounced enviable when compared with the condition of their brethren in the Pale of Settlement, where the rightlessness of the Jews during the period bordered frequently on martyrdom".[2]

The severity of anti-Jewish legislation was ameliorated, in the characteristic Russian way, by administrative inefficiency and corruption. Venal officials could often be bribed to enable Jewish traders to travel into forbidden provinces or a son to avoid conscription. There were also two periods, both under Tsar Alexander II, in which the Tsarist regime seemed to be liberalising. The first was in the 1850s and was brought to an end by the Polish revolt of 1863. During this period certain categories of Jews were allowed to live outside the Pale and Poland and conscription of child recruits ceased. The second was in the 1870s and was brought to an abrupt halt by the Tsar's assassination in 1881.

Although only one of the Tsar's assassins was of Jewish origin, this fact was enough to stimulate widespread pogroms, the first of which broke out in Kherson province in the Ukraine on 15th April 1881. There has been a long-standing Jewish view that these mob attacks were encouraged by the Tsarist state, but historians have found no evidence for this, although it seems undeniable that in some areas local officials sympathised with

---

2   Simon Markovich Dubnow, *History of the Jews in Russia and Poland,* Volume II, Jewish Publication Society of America, 1918, p.110 (reprinted by Filiquarian Publishing, 2011, p.62).

rioters and disturbances were woefully policed.[3] About 20,000 Jews had their homes destroyed and another 100,000 suffered major property loss.[4] The assassination and pogroms led to increased legal measures against Jews, most notably the so-called "temporary" laws of May 1882.

The new Tsar, Alexander III, was strongly influenced by Church officials, in particular his former tutor and chief procurator of the Holy Synod, Pobedonostsev, whose belief was that the gentile populace should be protected against the Jews and not, as one might have thought after a series of pogroms, the other way around.[5] The May Laws, drafted by the Minister of the Interior, Ignatiev, reinforced or supplemented existing anti-Jewish legislation in the Pale (but excepting Poland). Jews were prohibited from settling outside towns or owning land within the Pale of Settlement. And in those towns in which they were permitted to live, new measures came into force, which included prohibitions on Jews from transacting business on Sundays or on Christian holy days, giving plentiful scope for arbitrariness by local officials.[6] The May Laws were followed in subsequent years by other measures, including the introduction of Jewish quotas in schools and in the medical and legal professions.

3   Hans Rogger, *Jewish Policies and Right-Wing Politics in Imperial Russia,* Macmillan, Oxford, 1986, p.30 and p. 248 n. 70; I.Michael Aronson, "The Anti-Jewish Pogroms in Russia in 1881" in John D. Klier and Shlomo Lambroza (eds.), *Pogroms: Anti-Jewish Violence in Modern Russian History,* Cambridge University Press, Cambridge, 1992, pp. 52-3.

4   Alexander Orbach, "The Development of the Russian Jewish Community 1881-1903", in Klier and Lambroza (eds.), op.cit., p. 143.

5   Rogger, op.cit., p.67. Pobedonostsev is alleged to have said that the result of the new laws would be that: " one-third of the Jews will be forced to emigrate, another third will be compelled to accept baptism, and the remainder will starve to death". Whether he ever actually made this infamous remark, which is so often attributed to him, is now doubted (Rogger, op.cit., p. 261 n. 2).

6   Rogger, op.cit., pp. 59 - 62; J.D.Klier, "The Pogrom Paradigm in Russian History" in J.D.Klier and S Lambroza, op.cit., p.41.

It is part of the tradition of many Jewish families in the West that their forebears fled from Russia, in fear of their lives, to escape the pogroms that followed Tsar Alexander II's death. But while it is undeniable that the pogroms caused Jews from some localities to flee for self-protection, the greater significance of the pogroms (and new laws) in terms of Jewish history is their impact on the collective mind-set of the Jewish population of the Russian empire as a whole.[7] The pogroms were not general throughout Poland and the Pale. In some areas, like Lithuania, there were no pogroms at all. And emigration was not new. Emigration to the West had been increasing for decades. What news of the outrages did, followed by the oppressive absurdity of the May Laws, was to cause Jews in the Tsar's dominions to re-assess their lives and to think harder and more positively about emigration as a choice for themselves and their families. The increasing trend for individuals and families to leave for the West now accelerated into mass migration. As we shall see, David Applebaum was an early emigrant, whose departure *preceded* the great wave of emigration in the 1880s. However, his subsequent life and the life of his family was moulded by it and by the problems and opportunities it created.

What lay behind growing emigration to the West was demographic pressure. Without the complete emancipation of Russia's Jews, population growth would have generated greater emigration even had the Tsar never been assassinated. During the nineteenth century, Russia's Jewish population increased dramatically. In 1815, there were 1,200,000 Jews under Russian sovereignty; by 1897, the number of Jews had risen to 5,189,000 and might have been a million more but for emigration to the

---

7   John D. Klier. "Emigration Mania in Late Imperial Russia: Legend and Reality" in *Patterns of Migration 1850-1914,* Proceedings of the International Academic Conference of the Jewish Historical Society of England and the Institute of Jewish Studies, University College London, Aubrey Newman and Stephen W. Massil (eds.), Jewish Historical Society of England and the Institute of Jewish Studies, University College London, London, 1996, pp. 21-29.

West.[8] Throughout Europe, Jews tended to marry younger than gentiles. Marriages between boys of 15-18 and girls of 14-16 were common, with many Jewish girls producing children soon after puberty. In the Pale, however, perhaps the most significant demographic factor was that the Jewish death rate was less than half that of Russian Orthodox Christians.[9] A burgeoning Jewish population created pressure on available economic resources which was accentuated by legal restrictions on residence and occupation. The consequence was impoverishment, to the extent that by 1900 perhaps 20% of all Jews in some regions of Poland and the Pale were surviving on poor relief from other Jews.[10] Emigration was an answer: to central and to western Europe, to Argentina and South Africa, but most of all to *die goldene medina* ("the golden land", Yiddish), America.

8   Lloyd P. Gartner, *The Jewish Immigrant in England 1870 - 1914*, 3rd ed., Valentine Mitchell, London and Portland, Oregon, 2001 (first published 1960), p.21.

9   Paul Johnson, *A History of the Jews*, Weidenfeld and Nicholson, London, 1987, p.356; Rogger, op.cit., p. 235, n. 38.

10   Orbach, op.cit., p.141; Martin Gilbert, *Atlas of Russian History*, Dorset Press, USA, 1972, pp. 70-71.

3. Dobrin

Dobrzyn nad Wisla, that is, Dobrzyn on the Vistula river, is downstream from Warsaw, lying about 80 miles to the north-west of the Polish capital. Its current population is about 2,500. The Yiddish name for it was "Dobrin", for which the correct pronunciation is probably Dob-REEN,[11] and it is by this name that it will be referred to in this narrative. A British visitor in 2000 described Dobrin as a straggly town, running parallel to the river, and which consisted of "well-maintained mostly single-storey houses of brick or painted wood, some with corrugated iron roofs. There are few shops (no baker or butcher) and the main square was shaded by big trees, around which noisy dogs chased each other and unemployed men stared at us drunkenly".[12] There are no Jews in the town now. Its fine wooden synagogue [Ilustrations C and D] was burned down in the Second World War. The Jewish cemetery was also destroyed and the site now lies under water as a result of the damming of the Vistula for an industrial project.[13]

Dobrin in the nineteenth century seems to have been an undistinguished place [Illustration E], a dark, poor town with muddy streets, or so it is described in the *Yizkor* (Remembrance) Book for the larger, neighbouring town of Wloclawek.[14] Jews at one time made up a considerable proportion of the population of Dobrin, perhaps for a period a majority, and were engaged in a variety of trades and crafts. It was not a prosperous town, however, and during the nineteenth century emigration led to a halving of its Jewish population: down from 1,816 in1808 to 927 in 1897.[15]

---

11   Gabriel A Sivan, "They Sailed West; A Family Chronicle", *Shemot*, Vol.10,3, September 2002, p.22.

12   Judith Samson, "A Peek into the Polish Past", *Shemot*, Vol. 8,4, December 2000, pp. 25-6.

13   J. Preisler, *Memorial to the Destroyed Jewish Community of Dobrzyn nad Wisla, Poland*, www.jpreisler.com/dobrzyn (accessed 27th September 2011).

14   Preisler, ibid.

15   *The Encyclopedia of Jewish Life Before and During the Holocaust*, Shmuel Spector (gen.ed.), NYU Press, Jerusalem and New York 2001, Vol. 1, p.318.

Despite their declining numbers, the Jews of the town were a coherent community with a strong sense of local identity. This is seen from their capacity for mutual self-help after emigration. As was then common among emigrants, Jewish Dobriners formed *landsman* fellow country-man) groups for mutual support. These *landsmanshaftn* are known to have been set up in London, New York and Chicago.[16] In London, the group took the form of a friendly society, the Sons of Dobrin Benefit and Tontine Society. In due course, David Applebaum's eldest son, Maurice, became its president.

David Applebaum's actual date of birth is not known and 1855 is determined as the probable year by working back from the age given for him in the 1891 and 1901 British census returns and on his gravestone. It was a difficult time, for Russia was at war in the Crimea and Jewish conscripts were far away fighting and dying for the Tsar.[17] David's father's name was Manasseh. Who Manasseh's parents were and how they lived is unknown, but their choice of name for their son is intriguing. "Manasseh" is one of the so-called "epithetic names", a name given to express some real or imputed quality in the child to whom it is given. "Manasseh" means "he who make us forget" and was a name often given by parents after a family tragedy, for example, after the death of another child or at a time of family crisis.[18]

---

16   Preisler, op.cit.
17   In Sebastopol, there is a monument to the 500 Jewish soldiers who died in 1855 defending the besieged Crimean city against British and French forces (pictured on p. 159 of Yohanan Petrovsky-Shtern, *Jews in the Russian Army 1827-1917; Drafted into Modernity*, Cambridge University Press, New York, 2009). The monument's existence counters the anti-Semitic myth that Jewish soldiers did not fight as bravely for the Tsar as their Russian compatriots.
18   Genesis, Chapter 41, verse 51: "And Joseph called the name of the first-born Manasseh: For God, said he, hath made me forget all my toil, and all my father's house".

"Applebaum" is Yiddish for "apple tree". (The Yiddish word for an apple is "appel", not "apfel".) According to the Nahum Goldman Museum of the Jewish Diaspora in Tel Aviv, Jewish names deriving from "appel" are usually secular names stemming originally from the name "Abel", a diminutive of "Abba" or "Abraham". Most secular names were adopted by Jews for civil or business purposes from Hebrew or Yiddish names. Sometimes the secular names were taken or developed willingly; sometimes they were enforced by gentile authorities. In Britain, David Applebaum initially spelled his name "Appelbaum", but in the 1890s slightly anglicised the name to "Applebaum", which is how the surname is spelt in this narrative. Family members did not start to anglicise the surname more radically to "Appleby" until after 1900.

Manasseh Applebaum was a chandler, a manufacturer or supplier of candles.[19] These would have been tallow candles and may have included candles made from the fats of non-kosher animals, which some rabbinic authorities permit for certain purposes.[20] Whether he supplied the general market or Jews alone is not known, but he is sure to have had a niche market for candles used for Jewish religious purposes, such as Sabbath candles, which must burn with greater brightness than normal candles, or memorial candles or candles for the *Chanukah* (Festival of Lights) candelabrum, which must be of a special size or shape. This trade must by necessity have kept him close to Jewish religious life in Dobrin, which may have had an impact on the choice of career for his son, David.

---

19 Conversation with Lily Davidson, 3rd January 1989.
20 The instances in which it is permitted or forbidden under Jewish law to derive benefit from non-kosher items (in which the composition of candles is mentioned) are discussed in Rabbi Ari Z. Zivotofsky, *What's the Truth about...Kosher Soap,* www.oukosher.org/..../whats_the_truth_aboutkosher_soap (accessed 14th September 2011).

Manasseh Applebaum married twice, but we do not know the name of either wife. We know of four children of his first marriage, David and three sisters. Two younger sisters, called Sarah and Annie, were born in about 1860 and 1866 respectively and, like David, eventually emigrated to Britain. The third sister, whose name is currently unknown, seems to have stayed in Dobrin and, according to Annie Applebaum's granddaughter, Lily Davidson, was still there in the 1930s receiving clothes and food parcels and amounts of money sent from London.[21] One hopes this unnamed old lady died peacefully before the German invasion of 1939 and the horrors that followed. Manasseh's first wife died in about 1880 and he married again soon afterwards. The new wife did not warm to her step-daughter, Annie, and the girl was packed off to go to live with an uncle in Berlin. All that is known about the children of Manasseh's second marriage, some of whom he must have sired in his sixties, is that they included at least three sons and a daughter. These three sons all later emigrated to the USA, settling in Lexington, Mississippi.[22] Unlike

---

21   Conversation with Lily Davidson, 3rd January 1989.
22   The three brothers were called Sol (1882-1940), Nathan (1885 - 1939) and Abe (1890 - 1928). Sol came out first to Lexington and, after he had saved enough, brought over Nathan and Abe (letters from Karl Applebaum, 12th March and 29th July, 1989). He later established a thriving tailoring and cleaning business. Sol's son, Karl, came to the UK as a GI during the Second World War and managed to meet some British relatives after establishing contact by placing a newspaper notice. Since that time, almost seventy years ago, there are not known to have been any face-to-face contacts between the American Applebaums and their British relatives . The Jewish community in Lexington is described in a book by a one-time resident, Robert Lewis Berman, *A House of David in the Land of Jesus,* Robert Lewis Berman, USA, 2007. The Applebaum family businesses are mentioned on pp.171-2.

the British Applebaums, they kept the name "Applebaum", as did their descendants.[23] The only known daughter of the second marriage was born or later became blind and by the 1900s was living in France.[24]

23 Why did the "Applebaum" surname survive in the USA among Manasseh Applebaum's descendants, while in Britain they became "Appleby"? Perhaps it was because in the USA there was a greater tolerance of immigrant cultural difference. Or maybe it was because the far greater size of the Jewish population in the USA, by comparison with that in Britain, emboldened Jews to greater cultural self-confidence. A further reason may be that the Germanic-sounding nature of the name "Applebaum" made it relatively acceptable for use by Jews in a society where many of the gentile rich and powerful had Dutch or German surnames. As for Lexington, the Jewish community there was non-orthodox, keen to integrate and on the right side of the colour line. Robert Lewis Berman (ibid., p.241) is emphatic regarding the absence of anti-Semitism: " [it] was never manifested openly or surreptitiously, to the best of my knowledge, as a long- time resident with deep roots in the community. By all historical accounts, anti-Semitism did not exist and was never a problem in Lexington, past or present".

24 Letter from Karl Applebaum, 29th July 1989.

The language of David Applebaum's childhood home was Yiddish, as it was in the vast majority of Jewish homes in the Russian empire. Yiddish is a language based on medieval German city dialects which has absorbed Hebrew, Aramaic, Slavic and Romance elements. In the nineteenth century, it existed in broadly two forms: Western Yiddish (to the west of Poland) and Eastern Yiddish (Poland and eastwards), each subdivided into dialects. Eastern Yiddish, which reflected a much greater Slavic influence, was to form the basis for literary Yiddish, post-1870. Dobrin was situated in a transitional area between Western and Eastern Yiddish[25] and Dobriners spoke a more Germanic form of Yiddish than that spoken by Polish Jews further to the south and east. Dobrin was only 40 miles from the post-1815 Prussian border and had been part of Prussia between 1793 -1807. Even if this linguistic difference was only slight, David Applebaum and his family in later years spoke among themselves a more Germanised form of Yiddish than that spoken by many in the East End. David Applebaum's grandson, Basil Appleby, described it as *hoch* ("high") Yiddish.[26] A factor ccontributing to the use by the East End Applebaums of a more Germanic-influenced Yiddish would have been the family's experience in having lived in Germany for a period in the 1880s.

---

25   Eli Barnavi (ed.), *Historical Atlas of the Jewish People: from the Time of the Patriarchs to the Present,* Hutchinson, London, 1992, p.193.

26   Conversations with with Basil Appleby, 21st and 27th January 2009. Basil Appleby said he spoke his family's form of Yiddish well, but when taken as a child to a Yiddish theatre in London could not understand the Yiddish spoken on stage, although the rest of the audience could, which suggests that there was something different about the kind of Yiddish that the Applebaum family spoke. The author's father, Manny Appleby, spoke fluent Yiddish of a sufficiently Germanic quality for him to act as a translator for wounded German prisoners receiving medical treatment in British army facilities when he was a Royal Army Medical Corps orderly in the First World War.

Most Jewish men in Dobrin would by custom and necessity have been multilingual. Yiddish was the language of the household. Hebrew would have been learned and, to a lesser extent understood, as the language of prayer. Polish would be required to deal with gentile traders, customers or employees. Some Russian would have been known to deal with the authorities. Women, however, would have a more restricted linguistic repertoire. Only a minority would have any knowledge of Hebrew and many would have surprisingly little understanding of Polish if they did not work outside the home. There is no reason to believe that the Applebaum family was any different in these respects. David Applebaum's children, even those born in Britain, retained throughout their lives a high degree of fluency in Yiddish, which in some cases was transmitted to the next generation. As for Polish, whatever was known was largely forgotten after emigration and barely a word was passed on.

On the scant evidence available, it is likely that the Applebaums' Jewish neighbours regarded them as having attained a modestly comfortable standard of living. But these things are relative. In Dobrin, it may have taken very little to be considered prosperous. Conversely, to have been considered poor would have meant to be living a pretty wretched existence. We are on safer ground speculating about the Applebaums' religious life. They appear to have been a family that maintained traditional beliefs and practices without being excessively pious. We do not know whether or to what extent David Applebaum and his siblings and half-siblings received any secular education. If they did not, and had instead a traditional religious education, we can reasonably assume what this would have entailed.

The first school for Jewish boys from religious homes in Russia was the *cheder* (literally, the "room"), attended from about six. Moves to include Jewish girls within traditional education did not start until the end of the nineteenth century and then only in go-ahead places. For religious Jews, *cheder* was (and still is) a fundamental institution, which, in the words of one Jewish religious educationist, "emerged from the core of Jewish life...was created in the image of the community and became the people's pillar of strength".[27] It was intended to prepare a boy for his place in the community. Often divided into early childhood *cheder* and middle *cheder*, in the former a boy would learn to read Hebrew and in the latter study the *Torah* (the Pentateuch), Hebrew writing (the lettering also being used to write Yiddish), and customs relating to the synagogue and the home. Boys were placed in charge of a teacher, a *melamed*, a usually over-worked and under-paid family man, who might house the *cheder* in his own home.[28]

Modernisers regarded this old style religious schooling with dismay. According to the *Jewish Encyclopedia* of 1925,[29] "the *hedar* transforms healthy children into sulky and nervous ones and it has been said that the physical degeneration of the Jewish masses is due in part to the baneful influence of this kind of school." The *cheder* was further criticised for containing children of all ages in the same schoolroom, rendering systematic teaching impossible. Lesson time was said to be largely taken up by repetition out loud of Hebrew lessons. Schooldays took the whole day, six days a week, without summer vacations. Even if this view paints too dire a picture of traditional religious schools, it is clear that as an institution the nineteenth-century *cheder* failed to inculcate a reasonable level of literacy in Hebrew in many boys, who,

---

27   A.M. Lifshitz, quoted in Yaffa Eliach, *Once There Was A World: a 900-Year Chronicle of the Shtetl of Eishyshok,* Little, Brown and Company, Boston, New York and London 1998, p.147.

28   Eliach, op.cit., pp. 147-166.

29   *The Jewish Encyclopedia,* Isidore Singer (managing ed.), Funk and Wagnalls Company, New York and London, 1925, vol X, p.546.

as a consequence in adulthood, found difficulty in reading Yiddish newspapers or other material written in Yiddish.[30]

The last stage of the *cheder* was the *Gemara cheder*, where boys went to study the Talmud. Most boys never made it to this level of scholarship; they left to go into apprenticeship or to other work, which for many of the non-academic must have felt like a blessed escape. David Applebaum went through this stage of study and then on to a *yeshivah*, a traditional academy dedicated to a more thorough study of the Talmud and other rabbinical literature. A *yeshivah* was usually organised by a prominent scholar. Where David Applebaum attended is not known, although Appleby family lore maintains that he certainly did go to a *yeshivah*. Nothing about his adult life suggests, however, that he was a great scholar. Nor would this have mattered much. His fine voice and confident delivery must have been noticed early on, as a teenager in Dobrin. He is likely to have been something of a synagogue singing star, with all the congregation wondering and waiting to see how he might seize his chance in life.

---

30   Anne Kersten, "Yiddish as a Vehicle for Anglicization", in Klier and Lombroza, op.cit., p.60.

5. *Chazan, Schochet* and *Mohel*

David Applebaum's social standing in the Jewish communities in which he lived stemmed primarily from his various appointments as a *chazan*. He performed an important public communal function and, the larger and more well-known the synagogue in which he officiated, the more highly he would have been regarded. He was also a source of pride and status (*yichus*) to his family and relatives. It is remarkable that in the 1920s and 1930s a photograph of him in his formal robes stood in pride of place on a dresser in his half-brother Sol's house in Bible Belt Mississippi,[31] even though Sol, in his adult life, probably met his much older half-brother only once when passing through London on his way to America.

Since the destruction of the Second Temple, the Jewish religion has not possessed a priesthood, in the sense of a religious caste or elite with a wide, exclusive spiritual role. Among the orthodox, a rabbi is primarily a scholar and moral guide. His function is to be learned in Jewish law, to promote its study, to give rulings and advice, to act as a communal arbiter, and to provide an example to the community by living an upright life. In Poland in the nineteenth century, a rabbi might only preach in synagogue twice a year and then just to deliver a learned discourse on a religious subject. Routine preaching would be left to itinerant preachers, *maggidim*. The nature of synagogue services, lengthy, structured, repetitive, and with chanting, singing and ceremony, required a second, less learned and differently skilled religious functionary, the *chazan*, whose role it was to lead congregants though important parts of the service and, in particular, those where there was a musical element. Chanting and singing are an essential ingredient in orthodox Jewish worship. All readings from holy books require cantillation, a speech melody, a practice which is also followed by Muslims in the mosque

31   Letter from Karl Applebaum, 12th March 1989.

in their readings from the Koran. This is an ancient requirement of the Jewish faith, the singing of psalms and hymns evolving later.

The office of *chazan* is a long-standing one and has increased in importance over the centuries. A number of specific ceremonial duties were allotted to the *chazan*, including those relating to the bringing out and putting away of the scrolls of the Torah from the Synagogue ark, to readings from the scrolls, and to the blowing of the ceremonial ram's horn, the *shofar*. He might also supervise the synagogue chorus, the *mesharim*. His increasing importance corresponded with the decline in the knowledge of Hebrew among Jews of the dispersal and the development of musical elements in services. Someone was needed in synagogue services to guide the congregation through prayers and ceremonies, ensure correct Hebrew pronunciation and who knew and could tunefully render songs and chants. *Chazan* means overseer or director. In Britain, he was often called a "reader", a name which reflected the reality of diaspora life where the *chazan* might be one of only a few in the congregation with the Hebrew reading skills necessary to recite prayers quickly and with the accurate pronunciation. The name "cantor" is often used where the *chazan* is noted or specifically employed for his (and in the Reform Synagogue world, her) musical skills.

The traditional qualifications for a *chazan* were to have complete familiarity with Jewish liturgy, to be married, to live a life free from reproach and to have a pleasing appearance. He was also expected to be capable of a strong, melodious intonation, a tenor voice being generally preferred to a baritone or bass. It helped to possess stage presence and the sympathy of the congregation. The synagogue might be packed, the background hub-bub of congregants unrelenting, but a capable *chazan* would be expected to dominate the synagogue hall as he led the service with a powerful, expressive delivery.

Sometimes tensions could develop between a *chazan* and a synagogue's rabbi or its elected officers. *Chazanim* of the ordinary sort seem frequently to have felt underpaid. And the necessity that a *chazan* live his life free from any breach of religious law or breath of scandal was for many a challenge. However, for a *chazan* with a fine voice, many congregations would be forgiving. Love of religious music and of the theatrical elements in the synagogue service ran deep in traditional Jewish communities both in the homelands of Poland and the Pale and in the lands to which Jews emigrated. As far back as the Middle Ages, there were *chazanim* who were inclined to introduce into services melodies taken from non-Jewish sources. This was frowned on by purists, who sought simpler or more traditional tunes, but the tendency of *chazan*im to innovate was not checked. The desire of many *chazanim* was to seek as much latitude as was permissible to give their congregants musical pleasure in the course of their devotions. This might include the incorporation of coloratura, the musical frills, sometimes heart-rending in their plaintiveness, for which cantorial performance is famed.

By the late nineteenth century, a *chazan* with a superlative voice might become a celebrity, comparable to an operatic tenor, travelling widely, and developing a following beyond his own congregation. This trend became all the more marked with the development of sound recording. The first advertisements for gramophone records of cantorial performances appeared in the Jewish press in Britain in 1904.[32]

---

32   On 4th November 1904, The Gramophone and Typewriter Company Limited advertised in the *Jewish World* (p.115) a "Unique Series of Jewish Melodies comprising Ancient and Modern Chazonuth by the celebrated Cantor Sirota (of Wilna) and his Wonderful Choir". The newspaper was later moved to wonder whether "the gramophone will do for ...[the chazan]...what the motor threatens to do for the horse, relegate him to a museum of extinct species" (JW, 30th November 1904, p.273).

A "Golden Age of the Cantor" developed, particularly in the United States, with a small number of *chazanim* having their own managers who would take a percentage of their salaries to secure appointments.[33] Outside the synagogues, cantorial superstars performed on the secular stage. An example of this can be seen (and heard) in the 1929 "talkie", *The Jazz Singer*, where the famous cantor Yossele Rosenblat, known as the "Jewish Caruso", plays himself on stage with Al Jolson, both in the film and in reality the son of a *chazan*, in the theatre audience.

Less is known about David Applebaum's work as a *shochet* than about his activities as a *chazan* or a *mohel*. The work of a *shochet* is nevertheless more central to the life of a Jewish community than either of the other activities. Observance of the Jewish dietary laws, *kashrus*, is at the very heart of orthodox Jewish religious practice. It is an essential element of *kashrus* that only certain animals may be eaten - and these only if the animals have been killed in accordance with the Jewish law on animal slaughter, which is called *shechita*. If the rules of *schechita* are not observed then the flesh of even a permitted animal cannot be consumed. Without access to a *shochet*, therefore, a traditional Jewish community must go meatless.

It is the job of the *shochet*, a religious Jew trained and licensed to kill animals, either to slaughter animals himself or to certify as a *bodek* (examiner) that killings by another have been correctly conducted. Becoming a *shochet* required, and still requires, lengthy study and periodic examinations. An apprenticeship to a working *shochet* is required, which may be difficult to obtain, however. The number of religious Jews who require kosher meat may be small in any location

33   Velvel Pasternak, *The Jewish Music Companion,* Tara Publications, USA, 2002, pp. 58-63.

and, if the market for the work of a *shochet* is finite, as it usually is, he may only wish to provide apprenticeships to his sons or to the sons of close relatives.

We do not know where or when David Applebaum trained. He would have needed to learn the written law of *shechita*, animal anatomy and pathology, and the practical knowledge required to kill an animal and to "porge" (strip) a carcass of those parts of the hindquarters which it is forbidden to consume. The act of killing itself requires skill and attention to religious requirements. It must be undertaken with a single, quick, deep cut across an animal's neck with a perfectly sharp and undamaged blade. The method is intended to be painless and to cause unconsciousness to the beast within two seconds. It is a religious duty on the *shochet* to cause the minimum of suffering.

David Applebaum's third communal occupation was that of *mohel*. Taken together, the three activities require from a one person a remarkable range of disparate skills: the ability to intone melodiously and lead a congregation in prayer; the ability to kill large animals quickly and humanely; and the ability to conduct effectively, and in a calm and reassuring manner, an intimate operation on a baby boy during a joyful family gathering in the presence of the child's concerned parents. Nevertheless, Jewish communities frequently sought performance of all three functions by a single official. A small or poor congregation could not afford to pay a *chazan* a living wage for cantorial duties alone and it made sense to bundle up his job with other activities. These varied from synagogue to synagogue. In some places, a *chazan* might act as synagogue secretary, in others he might also act as schoolmaster. A young *chazan* with a growing family might not object to other duties if it meant better pay, although one does read of *chazanim* who found acting as a *shochet* disagreeable and sought to be released from this activity.

In the right context, working as a *mohel* could be the most remunerative of all three activities. It is a religious duty of the highest order on a Jewish father to ensure that his sons are circumcised.[34] Deaths after circumcision, an uncommon occurrence, were traditionally accepted as a consequence of the performance of this duty. Jewish law recognises this fact by providing that if two previous sons have died as a result of circumcision then a third son need not be circumcised, but will nonetheless be deemed circumcised for religious purposes.[35] It is a Jewish father's duty to perform the circumcision himself or to appoint a *mohel* to carry out the task. The ritual, a *bris millah*, must be carried out on the eighth day after the birth.

A *mohel* would be trained both in the understanding of the religious laws governing the ceremony and in its surgical aspects. The latter would include recognition of potential medical difficulties and supervision of post-operative care. Training would be by apprenticeship to a *mohel* and, once he gave his approval, a student could start to practice as an independent *mohel*. In the mid-nineteenth century in most of Europe, the training of a *mohel* involved much less modern medical content than today. Since the nineteenth century modern scientific medical understanding has been increasingly incorporated into the training of *mohelim*, most of whom are now medically qualified, and this has reduced the risk of surgical mishap and post-operative probelms. Another important factor in reducing risk has been the drive to encourage Jewish parents to engage only properly-trained operatives and follow their advice on post-operative care. But, as we shall see, many of the wave of poor Eastern European Jews who migrated westwards were too poor to do other than to instruct inexpensive, traditional *mohelim*, who were sometimes ignorant or careless.

---

34   Circumcision is a mark of the eternal covenant between God and the descendants of Abraham (Genesis, Chapter 17, verses 1-14; Leviticus, Chapter 12, verses 1-3).

35   *The Jewish Encylopedia*, Singer (managing ed.), op. cit., vol. IV, p.101.

6. Marriage

In April 1911, David Applebaum's widow told a British census-taker that she had been a married woman for 37 years. The information was conveyed through her eldest daughter, Sarah, because Mrs Applebaum's English was not very good. This places the marriage in 1874. David Applebaum would have been about 19 at the time and his bride one or two years older.[36] Her name was Shinah Leibah Martschin or Martchan and she used the non-Jewish first name "Jeanette" for dealings with the gentile world and, in Britain, anglicised her maiden name to "Marchant".

Jeanette, as she will be referred to in this account, was born in Dobrin. Her background was less esteemed than that of her husband. In later years, her daughter-in-law, Sadie Appleby, the wife of her son, Harry, used to say that her mother-in-law had no cause to give herself airs and graces as her family were "in the fish".[37] They were fishmongers, then, not a trade of which many East End Jews would have been especially proud, but, even so, they do not seem to have been poor. Jeanette's grand-daughter, Minnie Stein, nineteen at her grandmother's death, remembered seeing in her grandmother's house a silver candelabrum, cutlery and bedding which her grandmother said had been given to her on marriage by her parents; items that had travelled backwards and forwards across Europe with David and Jeanette since that time.[38]

Jeanette Applebaum showed great fortitude in her married life. She bore her husband fourteen children, twelve of whom survived until adulthood (Appendix A). Her growing flock, whom she herded between new homes

---

36   The precise age of David Applebaum's bride is not known. Counting back from the ages stated for her in the 1891, 1901 and 1911 British censuses gives dates of birth of 1854, 1856 and 1855 respectively. She died 1937. Her death certificate says she was 83 while her gravestone in Marlow Road Cemetery in East London provides an age of 84, giving dates of birth of 1854 and 1853 respectively.
37   Conversation with Elfrida Fine, 22nd September 1988.
38   Conversations with Minnie Stein, 11th August 1987, 12th October 1988.

during at least four long-distance house moves in twenty years, also included at times two of David's sisters, Sarah and Annie. In the domestic sphere, Jeanette would have been expected to exercise complete command over this entourage. She was able to do this with tolerable success during her husband's life, but far less so thereafter. She remained, nevertheless, up to her death in 1937, a matriarch revered, feted and deferred to by her family.

She was slim and was said to have been attractive in her youth. She was above average height for the time and brought a strain of reddish hair into the family. She never wore a *sheitel* (wig), as very pious married Jewish women do, although she was quite *frum* (religious). She liked to dress up and would insist on putting on a hat just to go to the corner shop. Two photographs of her survive, one taken in about 1925 and the other in the 1930s [Illustrations F and G].

David and Jeanette's first child, and the only child known to have been born in Poland, was a boy to whom they gave the name Moishe (Moses) and who later took the English name Maurice, as he will be referred to in this narrative. Born in Dobrin in about 1875,[39] he was to be the most successful of all their children, both financially and in terms of communal achievements. Maurice was also their only adult son who never went into or even dabbled in show business, as seven of his brothers did.

---

39   The exact date of the birth of Moishe Applebaum, who became Maurice Appleby, is also not known. He made two applications for naturalisation as a British citizen (National Archives reference: HO 144/999/126173 344459). In the first, made in 1905 and which he allowed to lapse, he gave a date of birth in 1876. In a second, made in 1911, and which was effective, he gave a date in 1874 (a date in 1876 having been originally inserted in his application and then crossed out to be replaced by the 1874 date). Counting back from his ages as given for him in the 1891 census and in his 1899 marriage certificate gives a date of 1875 in both cases. He cannot be found in the Ancestry.co.uk 1901 census database even though press reports in the *Jewish Chronicle* indicate that he was in London at about this time.

In the late 1870s, David Applebaum, his wife and son, turn up in London. The following period in their lives is obscure. All of the known facts about the family's stay in London at this time are contained in a single document; the birth certificate of the Applebaums' second son, Israel. The child was born on 17th December 1878 at "7 Wilks [sic] Street, Spitalfields", to "Davis Appelbaum" and his wife "Libra Appelbaum formerly Martchan". The occupation of the father is stated to be "Reader in the Synagogue". He is at this stage a 23 year-old man from a small town in rural Poland living with his family in the heart of the greatest city in the British empire. He would have spoken very little English and when exactly he arrived in London is unknown.

Emigration is often analysed in terms of "push" factors, which propel an emigrant to leave his home, and "pull" ones, which attract him to his destination. Dobrin was clearly a place which its Jewish inhabitants considered lacking in opportunity and which, throughout the nineteenth century, they readily left to better themselves. We know of eight children of Manassah Applebaum and of these seven emigrated (three to Britain, three to the USA and one to France) and only one remained in Dobrin. Another push factor for David Applebaum may have been the threat of compulsory military service.

The 1874 statute on military duty was intended to modernise conscription in Russia and so make the army more effective. Long periods of compulsory service were now shortened, but conscription was to be universal. Previous exemptions from conscription were be abolished, although sons who were a family's main breadwinner and Christian (but not Jewish) clergymen were not required to serve. As applied to Jews, administrative errors abounded in the enforcement of the new law. Blameless and dead Jews and even those actually serving in the army were listed as draft dodgers. The new statute had its first real test with the outbreak of the Russo-Turkish War of 1877-8, in which many conscripted Jews fought with heroism for the anti-Semitic Russian state,[40] while others fled the country to evade military service, some reaching London.[41] It is only speculation, but it is possible that among factors motivating David Applebaum to leave Dobrin was the desire to avoid entangling himself with the local draft committee.

London was not an obvious destination. David Applebaum had relatives in Berlin[42] and Jeanette's family may have had connections with America. Certainly, two of her brothers are said to have emigrated to Philadelphia.[43] Britain had the advantage of being en route to the United States, but it was not necessarily the first choice for Jewish emigrants. Among pious East European Jews, London's religious reputation was very low and British Jews were considered lax in observance and uninterested in religious study.[44] Nor was Britain viewed as a land of great economic opportunity. True, Jews there were free from the restrictions and obligations heaped on them in Russia merely for being Jewish and it was known that there were rich and powerful Anglo-Jews who rubbed shoulders with politicians and aristocrats. But a poor, new immigrant should expect that making a living in Britain would be hard and that gentile neighbours would be unfriendly.[45] Nevertheless, Jews came. Polish Jews had been arriving in London since the eighteenth

---

40   Pertovsky-Shtern, op. cit., pp. 129-134, 160.

41   Gartner, op. cit., p.40.

42   Conversation with Lily Davidson, 31st January 1989.

43   Conversations with Minnie Stein, 11th August and 21st September 1987.

44   David Feldman, *Englishmen and Jews: Social Relations and Political Culture 1840-1914*, Yale University Press, New Haven and London, 1994, p.351; Gartner, op.cit., pp. 29-30.

45   Gartner, op.cit., pp. 27-28.

century with their numbers increasing from the 1840s onwards.[46] Life was not going to be easy, they recognised, but it was likely to be better than back home.

David Applebaum probably chose to go to London in the 1870s simply because someone offered him a job there as a *chazan*. Israel Applebaum's birth certificate says his father was "Reader in the Synagogue", but it does not say which one and there were twenty or more in the vicinity at that time.[47] On the assumption that he left Poland to take up a job offer, there must have been someone in London, a sympathetic relative or family friend, who facilitated the offer and helped the young family with their move. Appointment as a *chazan* to any synagogue, even at a low salary, would have needed the support of synagogue members and in terms of synagogue politics, to bring to London a man in his early twenties and install him in post would have required the backing of a synagogue elder or someone else of influence. Attempts to find this person, the missing link as it were between Dobrin and London, have so far been fruitless. All that can be said is that available sources have not yet revealed anyone living in Spitalfields at the time who was clearly a *close* relative of David or Jeanette.

David Applebaum arrived in the East End before it became the East End. He arrived around 1877/8 and it was not until about 1880 that the term "East End" was coined.[48] It came quickly into general use and was as much a name for an idea as a place. It came to represent an urban extreme of squalor, poverty, disease, crime and hopelessness. But, as

46   Todd M. Endelman, *The Jews of Britain 1656 - 2000*, University of California Press, Berkeley, Los Angeles and London, 2002, p.128.

47   Gina Glasman, *East End Synagogues*, Museum of the Jewish East End, London, 1987, p.7.

48   W.J. Fishman, *East End 1888; a year in a London borough among the labouring poor*, Gerald Duckworth, London, 1988, p.1.

conditions improved and its inhabitants or their children moved on, so the idea of the East End became retrospectively sentimentalised. Other elements were added to the mix: the stubborn determination of the poor to survive, their resourcefulness and fierce family loyalty, their music and humour, and the exotic customs of new immigrants. Today, the nineteenth-and-early-twentieth century East End is a setting for fiction and fantasy almost as powerfully mythologised as the Wild West.

He also arrived well before the vast informal ghetto that became known as the Jewish East End reached its fullest flowering. In 1830, there had been about 20,000 Jews in London and by mid-century this number increased modestly to about 25,000. Most London Jews lived in the City or in the parishes on its immediate eastern side. During the 1860s and 1870s, the City declined as a residential area. Prosperous Jews moved out to suburbs to the west and north, but about two-thirds of London Jews remained in the old districts. By the time of the 1881 census, taken about a fortnight before the first post-assassination pogrom in Russia, there were about 46,000 Jews in London. This was the comparatively small Jewish London into which David Applebaum had come three or four years earlier. There were many middle class Jews, indeed the Jews of Britain at this time have been characterised as being mostly middle class,[49] but there were also many engaged in manual occupations or petty trading or who were simply paupers supported by Jewish charities. This antediluvian Anglo-Jewish world was transformed by a flood of immigration over the next quarter of a century. The new East European immigrants were poor, religious and alien to Anglo-Jewish ways. Their advent vastly increased the size of London's Jewish quarter. Between 1881 and 1900, the Jewish population of London rose from 45,000 to 135,000 and by 1914 it had risen further still to about 180,000.[50] In doing

49   Endelman, op. cit., p.79.
50   Geoffrey Alderman, *London Jewry and London Politics 1889-1986*, Routledge, London and New York, 1989, p.5, p.12; Endleman, op.cit., p.130.

so, the area of dense Jewish settlement expanded to the east and south, along the axes of Whitechapel Road and Commercial Road, shifting the centre of gravity of the Jewish East End from Spitalfields to somewhere just east of Gardiners Corner. At this date, no city in the world, other than New York or Chicago, contained more East European Jewish immigrants than London.[51]

Emigrants from Russia usually left for the west in the spring. Most did not have passports, which were expensive and not issued to potential conscripts. Those without passports relied on emigration agents who used subterfuge and bribery to get emigrants out of Russia. How much difficulty the Applebaum family faced is not known. They probably travelled by train to Berlin, by train again to Hamburg and then by steamship to Harwich or London. They were not among the poorest of migrants so it is possible that they were able to share a cabin for the slow voyage across the North Sea. Those with least money travelled steerage and after three days in overcrowded and unsanitary conditions would arrive dishevelled and exhausted at their port of disembarkation. Once in London, it is possible that 7 Wilkes Street was the young family's only home during their relatively short stay in the city. They would have lived as tenants in a single room or in two rooms at the most. The great metropolis would have been something of a shock to them; the foreign language, the noise of the city, the powerful industrial smells, the overcrowded houses and teeming streets, and the notorious London "particulars", the thick, sooty, throat-chafing, London fogs.

Wilkes Street ran north-south through Spitalfields and, since the Second World War, only the southern section, running south of Hanbury Street, remains. Number 7 lay in this southern section and has been demolished and re-built. It is, however, possible to get an idea of what the original

---

51   Gartner, op. cit., pp.16-7.

property looked like from surviving buildings, some of which have been lovingly restored. Dating from the 1720s, this part of Wilkes Street and some of the surrounding area of Spitalfields is now London's most complete enclave of early Georgian housing. The original houses in Wilkes Street were generally three storeys high, most with roof garrets and some with cellar-basements. Number 7 was a single-fronted end-of-terrace house, probably one room deep, which would have given it four rooms, assuming there was no inhabitable cellar. In the late 1870s, the narrow street must have been full of people for much of the day as residents spilled out of their overcrowded houses. Some idea of the degree of overcrowding can be gained from the 1891 census, when fourteen people comprised in three households are recorded as being crammed into number 7 Wilkes Street.

This part of Spitalfields had been occupied by French Huguenot immigrants in the eighteenth century, many of them silk weavers, but by the nineteenth century they had become assimilated or had moved on. The area became increasingly Jewish as the nineteenth century progressed, but it was not, by the late 1870s, as solidly Jewish as it was to become by 1914. The middle class nature of most of British Jewry prior to the great East European influx of the 1880s has been mentioned, but the Jews who lived in the vicinity of Wilkes Street at this time were definitely not middle class. Overwhelmingly, they were engaged in manual occupations or petty trading and about half of all Jewish breadwinners would describe themselves as tailors to 1881 census takers.[52] The area had by this time become predominantly

---

52   Data from the author's analysis of 1881 census responses of heads of households born in Russia (including Poland) and living in Hanbury Street. The 1881 census database available through Ancestry.co.uk contains no data on certain streets in Spitalfields, including Wilkes Street, Fournier Street and Puma Court, because these streets were omitted from the census (see Note on Sources and Select Bibliography, below).

Polish Jewish. There had been a sizeable community of Dutch Jews in Spitalfields since mid-century, but these economic migrants from the Netherlands became increasingly outnumbered by Polish Jews. They were not generally Yiddish-speaking and David Applebaum would have been surprised to find some fellow Jews in Spitalfields with whom he could barely communicate, he speaking little English and they speaking little Yiddish.

The young Applebaum family cannot have found life financially easy. An insight into what David Applebaum might have earned may be gathered from a row that broke out at the nearby small Princes Street Synagogue in the 1870s. In 1873, the synagogue had advertised for a reader at a salary of £50 a year. By 1876, the then reader, Reverend Cohen, was receiving £60 a year and an attempt was made at the annual meeting of the synagogue to raise this salary to £100 a year. A resolution was moved and was defeated. Reverend Cohen either then resigned or was discharged; however, shortly afterwards, peace was made between synagogal factions and he was reinstated.[53] We may infer then that David Applebaum earned about a pound a week. This was less than the wages of an ordinary office clerk or a dockworker in continuous employment. A pound a week is also what the fictitious *chazan* Greenberg received in Israel Zangwill's 1892 novel "Children of the Ghetto". For Greenberg, his low salary was source of grievance and he complained constantly about his poverty.[54] The Applebaums would have been hard pressed, although a pound a week was just enough for a family of three to live on if they were frugal, teetotal and rented only a single room, for which the rent

53   Samuel C. Melnick, *A Giant Among Giants*, Pentland Press, Durham, 1994, pp. 43-47. Princes Street was later renamed Princelet Street and the *shul*, in consequence, became Princelet Street Synagogue.
54   Israel Zangwill, *Children of the Ghetto; A Study of a Peculiar People*, first published 1892, reprinted, William Heinmann, London, 1922, p.116.

would have been about five shillings (25p) a week. It is likely that by this stage David Applebaum had already trained as a *shochet* and it is possible that he was able to supplement whatever he earned as a *chazan* with earnings from slaughterhouse work; however, it is also possible that his employing synagogue expected him to carry out the work of a *shochet* for no additional salary, which was the fate of the unhappy Greenberg in Zangwill's novel.

Even if David Applebaum earned just enough for his family to get by, how happy would he and his wife and children have been in the milieu they inhabited? Urban social problems were general throughout the East End, but some streets were worse than others and adjoining streets or different ends of the same street might have a quite different character from each other. Brick Lane south of the railway lines was Jewish but to the north it was gentile. The southern end of Wilkes Street seems to have been fairly salubrious, by East End standards, but a hundred yards away was "Itchy Park", the churchyard of Christchurch, where scabrous vagrants congregated. A hundred yards beyond that was Flower and Dean Street, filled with common lodging houses, where street prostitutes of the poorest and most wretched sort paid a few pence to spend the night. Spitalfields was to become the heartland of the Jack the Ripper story. Number 7 is less than a hundred yards to the south of the place where they found the body of the Ripper's second victim (Annie Chapman, 8th September 1888) and two hundred yards north of the murder location of the Ripper's fifth (Mary Jane Kelly, 9th November 1888). At night, alleys and courtyards were unlit. In the streets, illumination from gas lights was often inadequate. It was not an area in which a decent woman would walk alone at night or choose to bring up her children.

In 1880 or 1881, David and Jeanette had a third son, who came to be called Hyman. His birth was never registered and his date of birth is inferred from his age as given in subsequent censuses and in his marriage certificate. There is little doubt that he was actually born in London; this is what census takers were later told and what is stated in his British army records.[55] His Hebrew name was probably Chaim, but he seems to have been called Hyman from early childhood. In the same way, his elder brother Israel, came to be called Isidore. The fact that Hyman's birth was not registered is significant. The Applebaums were not punctilious about legal formalities but they generally did what was required by the law. It is quite likely that the birth was not registered because as soon as the child and its mother were able to travel the Applebaums left the country believing that they might never come back . We can only guess at why they left. They may have been tired of Spitalfields or it may be that David Applebaum's contract as *chazan* had come to an end. It is possible that he felt the need to go back to Poland because his mother was dying or because she had died and his father was now re-marrying, events which happened about this time. Most likely they left because he had been offered a better job elsewhere.

---

55   Counting back to establish the date of birth for Hyman Applebaum on the basis of the age in years provided by or for him gives the following dates : 1891 census - 1880, 1901 census - 1881, 1906 marriage certificate -1881, 1911 census - 1880. His army records state he was born in Stepney, but this is thought to have been unlikely. He lived in Stepney at the time he went into the army in 1916 and may have given Stepney as his place of birth because he was unaware of the actual location. In 1880/1, Stepney was not yet a Jewish area and would have been an inconvenient place to live if David Applebaum was working in what was then the core Jewish area of Spitalfields.

During the early 1880s, the Applebaums were living in Germany. If their stay in London from 1887/8 - 1880/81 is mysterious, the period they spent in Germany, perhaps four or five years, is beyond that; it is almost a blank page. No German documents relating to it have so far been located.

David Applebaum, his wife and three sons, left either London for Poland, and then went from there at some later date to Germany, or went straight to Germany. While in Germany, David and Jeanette had three daughters: Rose, Sarah and Annie. The girls' place of birth is given as "Lauttenburg" in the 1901 British census and as "Lautenburg" in the 1911 census. Their dates of birth can be reckoned by counting back from the ages given for them in later British documents. On this basis, Rose's approximate date of birth was 1882/3, Sarah's 1884/5 and Annie's 1885/6.[56]

There are various candidates for the German town in which the Applebaums settled. By far the best is a small town called Lautenburg, at that time just ten miles from the Russian border. The town is now the Polish town of Lidzbark, known as Lidzbark Welski, to distinguish it from nearby Lidzbark Warminski. In the 1880s, it was part of the German Empire and before unification in 1871 it had been part of the kingdom of Prussia. The town is situated in that region of Germany which was ceded to Poland in 1918 and which became known as the Polish Corridor, although it is more properly referred to as West Prussia. The town is only

---

56   The dates of birth which can be inferred from the ages given in later British
     documents for each the three daughters born in Germany are as follows:
     Rose: 1891 census - 1882; 1901 census - 1883; 1911 census - 1882;
     Sarah: 1891 census - 1884; 1901 census - 1885; 1911 census - 1885;
                  1915 marriage - 1884;
     Annie: 1891 census - 1886; 1901 census 1886; 1911 census 1884;
                  1917 marriage - 1885.
     As a general rule, the younger an individual, the more likely it is that the age
     provided to a census taker for them will be accurate.

50 miles as the crow flies from Dobrin, at that time on the other side of the German-Russian border, but its character was different. Dobrin lay in the flat, fertile region of the Vistula valley, while Lautenburg was in an area of thick forests, lakes and low hills. Lautenburg was probably the more prosperous of the two roughly similar-sized towns. It had forges, saw mills, breweries and water mills and was soon to be linked to the outside world by railway, an amenity which, to this day, Dobrin has never possessed. Lautenburg was also a local administrative and legal centre and, by comparison with Tsarist Dobrin, government officials in Prussian Lautenburg could be expected to be more efficient and less corrupt.

The population of the town on the arrival of David, Jeanette and their three boys was about 3,500, of whom about 450 were Jews.[57] The gentile population was split between German and Polish speakers. The region had been seized by Prussia from Poland in 1772 and, since then, Polish-speakers had been subjected to a policy of Germanisation and German-speaking colonists had been settled among them. By comparison with Dobrin, the place was less Jewish, although there were quite enough Jews to support a self-governing *Kehillah* (council) through which Jews organised their communal affairs. David Applebaum must have come to Lautenburg to take up a job as a *chazan*. How he got the job is unknown. It is remarkable that at a time when thousands of Jews from Russia were streaming westwards, he and his family were migrating eastwards so that he could take up work in a West Prussian border town. It points up the highly mobile lives *chazanim* and their families lived; they went where the work was. This meant being prepared to move to sometimes remote or obscure Jewish communities provided the communities were large enough and prosperous enough to be able to support a synagogue *chazan*. It seems likely that while in Lautenburg David Applebaum

---

57   *Encyclopedia of Jewish Life*, op.cit., Vol.2, p.728, states that the Jewish population of Lautenburg reached a peak of 489 in 1885.

started to practice as *mohel*. In a court case in 1904, he stated that he had been practising as a *mohel* for 22 years, which would date the start of his practice to 1882, about the time he and his family established themselves in Lautenburg.

The Jewish community in Lautenburg was not however to prosper. Migration to larger towns in Germany and emigration abroad, both voluntary and forced, reduced the Jewish population of Lautenburg to 60 by the early 1920s.[58] The area also suffered by being in a war zone during the few weeks of the First World War and again in 1920 during the Polish-Soviet war. Most Jews who left during these periods of insecurity never came back. Today, all that remains of Jewish Lautenburg is a score of broken tombstones in the vandalized Jewish cemetery, a virtual walking tour of which is available on the internet.[59]

The Applebaum family's stay in Germany lasted only a few years and the question must be asked again as to how they came to move on; push or pull? Lautenburg, a small country town with clean air and open countryside near at hand, must have seemed a pleasanter place to raise a family than their previous home in Spitalfields. Why then should they leave? It is possible that they did so for purely economic reasons. David Applebaum 's contract may have come to an end or he may have found his existing level of pay unsatisfactory, now he had more mouths to feed. However, there is evidence that he left as a result of official pressure. Jews in Germany had finally become emancipated by the new Reich Constitution of 1871. They had therefore broadly the same legal rights as gentiles, although this did not stop them facing more anti-Semitic political agitation and general prejudice than did their counterparts

---

58   Ibid.
59   www.sztetl.org.pl/.../lidzbark.../10423, jewish-cemetery-in-lidzbark. (accessed 29th February 2012).

in Britain.[60] Still, Germany was a far better place for a Jew to live than Russian Poland. But life was only secure for Jews from Russia who settled in the former kingdom of Prussia if they had become naturalised German citizens. If they had not, then from the mid-1880s, they faced the threat of deportation.

Russian Jews had been migrating to Germany for decades. These would have included the Applebaums' relatives in Berlin. During the 1880s, the flow of Jewish immigration increased, although the number of alien Jews in Prussia was far exceeded by that of immigrant Poles of Russian nationality. Many of the Poles were agricultural workers, employed on the great estates of Prussian junker landlords. In March 1885, the German Chancellor and Minister-President of Prussia, Prince Otto von Bismarck, ordered the expulsion of all Russian Poles and Jews. The edict was not prosecuted with uniform rigour throughout Prussia; nevertheless, tens of thousands were forced to leave Prussia. Much hardship was caused and stories abounded of families being broken up, of immigrants being roughly handled and of humble Polish farm workers being forcibly ejected at the Russian border in the depths of winter by Prussian gendarmerie. The manner of the expulsions led to an outcry internationally and, in Germany, to protests within liberal circles and condemnation by the Reichstag.[61]

Within Prussia, for example in Memel and Konigsberg,[62] Jews who were German nationals formed committees to assist their alien co-religionists. Many Polish Jews had no wish or were scared to return to Russia. These were helped to emigrate westwards, to the USA, Britain

---

60   Endelman, op. cit., p.153.
61   Vejas Gabriel Liulevicius, *The German Myth of the East: 1800 to the Present*, Oxford University Press, Oxford, 2010, p.103.
62   *JC*, 25th September 1885, p.13; *JC*, 13th November 1885, p.11.

or the Netherlands. A large number ended up in Britain and in February 1886 the Chairman of the Jewish Board of Guardians, the principal charitable body among British Jews, declared publicly that the large increase in Jewish immigration over the previous year was attributable to expulsions from Prussia.[63]

In March 1885, Prussian authorities also announced that all Jews of Russian citizenship who held clerical appointments must vacate their offices.[64] The Kaiser was petitioned on behalf of many of these unfortunate clergymen and a surprising number of these petitions were reported to have succeeded.[65] Even so, many clergymen had to leave and some came to Britain, where the fortunate found work with sympathetic congregations. We read in the *Jewish Chronicle* of two *chazanim* from West Prussia who found work in Britain at this time.[66] Reverend Rutowski, formerly of Konitz, was appointed first reader of the Liverpool *shul* in August 1885. Reverend Jospe, formerly of Strasburg, only 20 miles from Lautenburg, was in February 1886 engaged to conduct services at the Princes Street Synagogue in one week and at the Hambro Synagogue the week following. Reverend Applebaum would have been in much the same position as these gentlemen. He was a Russian national, as he was to remain for the rest of his life. He would have been under the threat of expulsion and may even have been deported. That he should return to Britain in 1886 must have some connection with the Bismarckian expulsions taking place at exactly the same time. It is unlikely to have been just a coincidence.

---

63   *JC*, 12th February 1886, p.7
64   *JC*, 6th March 1885, p.7.
65   *JC*, 9th July 1886, p.13.
66   *JC*, 21st August 1885, p.1; *JC*, 5th February 1886, p.1; *JC*, February 12th 1886, p.2.

With the arrival in Newcastle upon Tyne of David and Jeanette Applebaum, together with their six children and, it is believed, his younger sister Annie, the Applebaums step out of the shadows into historical light. This is a reflection of the existence of a lively British-Jewish press and the editorial policies it pursued. The main newspaper for British Jewry was the *Jewish Chronicle*, published since 1841, and joined in 1873 by a rival, the slighter and, in its earlier years, more populist *Jewish World*. From the late 1870s, the *Jewish Chronicle* pursued a policy of being less London-centric and of carrying more news stories on Jewish life in the provinces. It also started to contain more news regarding communal life in the small East End synagogues used by recent immigrants.[67] As a result, from 1886 to David Applebaum's death in 1907, the occasional passing references to him in the *Jewish Chronicle* and, to a lesser extent, the *Jewish World* enable us to track his career. Later, when his eldest son Maurice became a significant figure in the Jewish friendly society movement, a similar stream of brief mentions is available.

We can assume that the Applebaums again left via Hamburg, but this time their port of disembarkation is likely to have been Hull. If so, there was a train journey to be made to Newcastle. The community which David Applebaum was to serve may have sent a Yiddish speaker to Hull to meet the Applebaums and travel with them to Newcastle or perhaps someone from the Hull Jewish community was deputed to meet them and put them on the right train. A number of bulky family possessions were shipped separately. David Applebaum's grand-daughter, Minnie Stein, recollected that they brought over from Germany good quality furniture and feather mattresses.[68] As the Applebaums travelled north, they would have passed first through pleasant countryside and historic

---

67   David Cesarani, *The Jewish Chronicle and Anglo-Jewry 1841-1991*, Cambridge University Press, Cambridge, 1994, pp. 65, 68-9.
68   Conversation with Minnie Stein, 12th October 1988.

towns, then through an area of intense coal mining, the like of which they had probably never seen before, finally arriving at the bustling and dynamic city of Newcastle.

Newcastle expanded rapidly in the nineteenth century, its population increasing eightfold (1801 - 28,000, 1831 - 53,000, 1851 - 87,000, 1901 - 215,000). As a port situated in the North-East coalfield, it had long been a centre of the coal trade. Now it was to become known for ship building and heavy engineering. The Applebaums arrived in a period of great civic improvement. As the town grew in size, it modernised. In the first half of the century, the town centre was rebuilt; in the second half, new middle class suburbs were established. In the 1870s, the first public parks were opened. In 1876 Newcastle's hydraulic swing bridge began to accept road traffic and in 1879 the first horse-drawn trams ran in Newcastle's streets. And, to reinforce Newcastle's greater importance, the Church of St Nicholas became a cathedral in 1882 and Newcastle could properly be referred to thereafter as a city. Although much of Newcastle was smoky, grimy and congested, it was alive with opportunity for the industrious and the lucky.

As Newcastle grew, so did its small Jewish community. Of Britain's 60,000 Jews in 1880, about 15,000 lived outside London. The largest community in the North-East was Newcastle, with outlying communities in Sunderland, Middlesborough, West Hartlepool and South Shields. Modern Jewish settlement in Newcastle dates back to the late eighteenth century. By 1838, a synagogue had opened in Temple Street. Between 1845 and 1880, the number of Jews in Newcastle rose from 33 to 750.[69] During this period of growth, two separate congregations came into being, chiefly as a result of the community outgrowing the Temple

---

69   Lewis Olsover, *The Jewish Communities of North-East England 1755-1980*, Ashley Mark, Gateshead, 1980, pp.12, 29.

Street Synagogue. In the 1870s, the two congregations agreed to unite and fund raising began to acquire land and construct a new and larger house of worship. The new synagogue, in Albion Street, later to become Leazes Park Road, was consecrated in August 1880 by Reverend Dr Hermann Adler, the son and deputy of the Chief Rabbi, Nathan Adler. The consecration was followed by a banquet and ball, as befitted the successful outcome of an ambitious project. Land had been acquired cheaply, but the costs of construction were considerable, given the limited resources of the community. Despite assiduous fund raising (Messrs Rothschilds donated 200 guineas), the community now had a mortgage of £3,500 on its books, which, as its elected officials were well aware, would weigh heavily and limit the capacity of the congregation to expand communal activities for many years to come.[70]

The United Congregation, as it was now called, had a fine *shul* to show for its efforts. Leazes Park Road is narrow, but the facade of the synagogue is impressive (Illustration J). The *Jewish Chronicle*'s correspondent attending the consecration, in a remarkable outpouring of architectural detail, described it as:

> *"...pure Byzantine. The walls of the building are of a composite character, built with rubble and blockstone dressings, from quarries in the district. The front of the building ...is more than 80 feet long, and has six piers in its length, enriched with bands, string courses, and capped with ornamental turrets, with angle columns and terminals. The principal entrances have moulded and carved labels, with carved and perforated tympans, moulded jambs, transoms, and angle shafts. The windows are finished with moulded heads and divided into lights by piers and columns, those*

---

70   As late as 1903, there was still £2,500 of the debt outstanding (*JW*, 30th January 1903, p.340).

*of the gallery floor have circular heads and the spandrils enriched
with geometrical carving. The centre of front is finished with a high
gable. The back gable, having a fully moulded coping and parapet,
is supported by moulded corbals. The back gable and the Ark is
perforated with a large half-wheel window of dressed stone fitted
with original painted glass of the most exquisite design..".*[71]

The building ceased to be used as a synagogue in 1978. When visited by
the author in 2008, it had become a bar and comedy club.

At the time that Dr Adler was opening the Synagogue, the Applebaums
were probably still living in Wilkes Street. The character of the small Jewish
community in Newcastle was different from that in Spitalfields, with a
greater proportion of Newcastle's Jewish population being engaged in
trading activities rather than manual occupations. A means of livelihood
frequently pursued by Jews in the North-East was that of credit draper.
New immigrants would set themselves up as pedlars or hawkers, either on
their own account or as agents for others, selling haberdashery, shoelaces,
cheap jewellery, sponges or wash leathers, door-to-door or in markets.
Once sufficient capital had been generated, margins could be increased by
selling on credit or perhaps a shop might be rented. Other common trading
activities for Newcastle Jews were pawnbroking and furniture retailing. It
was a small, hardworking community, which had striven to integrate and
which was generally accepted. At the Newcastle synagogue's consecration
in 1880, the Sheriff of Newcastle, two aldermen and members of local
municipalities attended. When it was re-consecrated in 1893, the mayor
came, together with the president of the British Medical Association, who
happened to be in town, "both attired in their official robes".[72]

71   *JC*, 27th August 1880, p.6.
72   *JC*, 8th September 1893, pp. 16-17.

The community in Newcastle continued to grow, reaching about 1500 in 1890 and 2500 in 1910.[73] The new synagogue became the centrepiece of a self-confident community, which, by the end of the century, had developed a range of communal institutions, including a Jewish Board of Guardians (for "relieving the poor and granting loans"), a Jewish school, charitable, burial and benefit societies, cemeteries, a literary society and a working men's club. Its members initially lived near the Synagogue in the city centre in such streets as Westmorland Road, Temple Street and Charlotte Square, but, as the century drew to a close, many of the Jewish better-off moved to the more desirable Jesmond area.[74]

The character of the Jewish community was, however, to change. It was affected in the same way as Jewish communities elsewhere in Britain by the influx of poor, Yiddish-speaking immigrants from Russia post-1881. The expansion of the Newcastle community in following years owed more to increased immigration than to natural growth. A question to be asked is whether this inflow of foreign Jews led to any lessening in gentile acceptance of the community. It has been observed that there was a distinct heightening of anti-Jewish feeling in Britain during the last twenty years of the nineteenth century.[75] It is unlikely that Newcastle would have been completely immune to changes in the national mood; however, there is no evidence for this in the period during which the Applebaums lived in the city. News stories about the Newcastle Jewish community in the *Newcastle Daily Chronicle*, were respectful and sympathetic[76] and in 1890 editorials and articles in the

---

73   Olsover, op.cit., p. 178
74   Olsover, op.cit., pp. 78, 127-133, 128, 134-141,143, 173.
75   Cesarani, op.cit., p.82.
76   For example, NDC, 22nd June 1887, p.4; 20th January 1888, p.5; 5th March 1888, p.4. An example of sympathetic article in a Newcastle local newspaper some years later is cited in the *Jewish World* of 4th January 1901, p.242.

newspaper attacked the latest anti-Jewish laws in Russia in the strongest language. The Tsar's policy was a "barbarity". It was "a disgrace in an age of civilisation" and "as diabolical a policy as has ever entered the human brain".[77] In these matters, the editorial line taken by the city's daily newspaper is unlikely to have diverged dramatically from the general attitude of its readers. It was certainly a view which resonated with the city's gentile mayor, who in May 1891, in making a presentation on behalf of the Newcastle congregation to its outgoing minister, and as paraphrased by the *Jewish Chronicle*, spoke with powerful fellow-feeling regarding the plight of Russian Jews:

> "*Persecution in many parts of the world against...[the Jews] ...was more severe and rampant than ever...and if there was ever a time when they should expect that they will receive the sympathy and that justice which humanity demanded, these were the times in which they live in now. (Applause). They had not to bear and suffer in Newcastle what their fellow Jews had to suffer in other parts of the world. (Applause). Whether it was because the Newcastle people were more Christian than others, or whether they knew and felt that they, like themselves, were God's children it was not for him to say, but he, representing the people of Newcastle and as Mayor of the city, deemed it a great honour to be present on that occasion (Applause)...*".[78]

---

77   *NDC*, 31st July 1890, pp.4 and 5; 4th August 1890, p.4. Additionally, in its 1st August 1890 issue, the newspaper carried a long letter from Mr C. S. Sherman, curate of St. Paul's church in Newcastle, vigorously attacking new Russian anti-Jewish laws: "...the whole thing is infamous; it is revolting to true Christianity; it is antagonistic to the mind of Jesus Christ..." (p. 5). The plight of Jews in Russia at this time received much sympathy in Britain; however, the expressions of support recorded in the Newcastle local press seem to have been unusually strong.

78   *JC*, 22nd May 1891, p.9

The position of Newcastle Jewry should be compared with that of another provincial Jewish community, Leeds, eighty miles away. The Jewish community in Leeds was younger than its sister community in Newcastle, yet it grew much more quickly and by 1900 was five times the size of Newcastle, numbering 10,000-12,000 people. At that time, 72% of employed Jewish adults in Leeds were engaged in the production of tailored garments, working in overcrowded, dirty and unsanitary workshops each employing on average 25-35 hands. Most of the Leeds Jewish population were concentrated in the poor Leylands district of central Leeds, which has been described as a ghetto.[79] Jewish immigrants gravitated to the sweatshops and to the dingy terraced streets of Leylands because they had little alternative when faced with "no Jews need apply" in their efforts to find work and accommodation. The years of heavy Jewish immigration into Leeds were marked by running fights in Leylands, especially on pay day, when drunk or bored groups of gentile young men, often armed with sticks or clubs, would invade the neighbourhood to harass or pick fights with Jews.[80] Problems continued into the new century. In 1906, a local newspaper was accused of giving too much prominence to anti-Semitic letters and carrying too many of them.[81] A year later, a newly-opened café in the city centre was refusing to serve Jewish customers and a petition was being circulated against a new Jewish chief medical officer.[82] Hostility in Leeds towards immigrant

---

79   E.Krausz, *Leeds Jewry: its History and Social Structure*, Heffer & Sons, Cambridge, 1964, p.6, p.17.

80   Murray Freedman, *Leeds Jewry – The First Hundred Years*, Leeds Branch of the Jewish Historical Society of England, York, 1992, p.12; Colin Holmes, *Anti-Semitism in British Society 1876-1939*, Holmes & Meier Publishers Inc, New York, 1979, p.110.

81   *JW*, 14th September 1906, p.403; *JW*, 28th September 1906, p.447.

82   *JW*, 21st June 1907, p.18; *JW*, 26th July 1907, pp.7, 18; *JW*, 2nd August 1907, p.18.

Jews reached a climax during the First World War, culminating in three-days of anti-Semitic rioting in June 1917.[83]

There was nothing comparable to this in the North-East. Newcastle was bigger than Leeds and had fewer Jews. And although there was a small Jewish quarter in central Newcastle, there was no concentrated Jewish presence on the scale of Leylands. The influx of Jews to Newcastle post-1881 may have ruffled local gentile sensibilities less than in Leeds simply because there were fewer Jewish immigrants and the community they were joining was smaller. Additionally, the occupations pursued by many Newcastle Jews were less likely to generate feelings of otherness towards them than those typically followed by the Jews of Leeds. The Jewish credit drapers and shop owners of Newcastle interacted face-to-face with the host community daily and there was less scope for irrational prejudice and hostility being directed towards them than against Jews in the self-contained world of tailoring sweatshops in Leeds (and where the tailors and pressers pursued occupations which many English working men considered unmanly[84]). A further explanation might be added. The North-East at this time, unlike some other areas of country, was used to receiving and assimilating Scottish and Irish immigrants and does not appear to have been overly hostile to strangers. An influx of Irish after the great famine of 1846-7 raised the Irish-born population of the Newcastle to 8% by 1851. By 1874, only three other towns in England had more Irish-born inhabitants. These seem to have been easily absorbed into local working-class communities.[85]

83   Freedman, op.cit., p.12; Holmes, op.cit., Holmes & Meier Publishers, New York, 1979, p.110ppp.130-1. The pretext for rioting was the reluctance of immigrants who were not British nationals, and who could not therefore be conscripted, to volunteer to fight.
84   Feldman, op. cit., p.285.
85   David K Renton, *Newcastle; City of Migration*, www.dkrenton.co.uk/newcastle.html (accessed 19th February 2012).

The years during which David Applebaum lived and worked in Newcastle were regarded by his family after his death as the zenith of his career. As reader of the Newcastle *shul*, he was not only a prominent figure among local Jews, he would also have been regarded as a person of some standing within the wider community. On his death, his family ensured that a reference to his time as reader at the Newcastle synagogue appeared on his gravestone and in the years that followed his sons would claim a worthy pedigree by reference to his Newcastle appointment. To them, it was the most notable thing their father ever achieved.

In April 1886, Reverend Solomon Jacobs, minister of the Newcastle congregation, left to take up a post in Jamaica, to be replaced by Reverend S. Friedberg, and at about the same time, Reverend Moses Claff, the reader since September 1884, departed for a similar position with the Princes Street Synagogue in London.[86] He was replaced by David Applebaum. The post of reader, unlike that of minister, does not appear to have been advertised, which suggests that Reverend Applebaum was appointed as a result of a recommendation, but by who is not known.

David Applebaum is first mentioned in the *Jewish Chronicle* in relation to a wedding on 1st September 1886 at the Newcastle Synagogue at which he and Reverend Friedberg officiated. It seems to have been a big occasion; a local Newcastle girl marrying a gentleman from London.[87] David Applebaum would have been hired in time for autumn festivals of *Rosh Hashonah* (Jewish New Year) and *Yom Kippur*, but there is no mention in the *Jewish Chronicle* of him officiating in Newcastle on these occasions. This was left to the newspaper's competitor, the *Jewish*

---

86   *JC*, 12th September 1884, p.12; *JW*, 9th April 1886, p.1 (the minister's salary in Newcastle was advertised at £78 p.a., "which can be greatly augmented"); *JC*, 16th April 1886, p.13; *JC*, 30th September 1887, p.11.

87   *JC*, 10th September 1886, p.1.

World.[88] The newspaper reported that on *Rosh Hashonah* and *Yom Kippur* the Newcastle synagogue was so crowded that, although capable of seating 520, extra chairs had to be found for additional numbers. The Reverend S. Friedberg delivered sermons and prayers were read by Reverend David Applebaum. The novelty of having both a new minister and a new *chazan* must have helped swell synagogue attendance on these holy days.

David Applebaum was employed by the Newcastle congregation in the triple capacity of *chazan, shochet and mohel,* which was the Newcastle synagogue's practice. It is not clear whether his salary was inclusive of any payment for circumcisions. What evidence there is from other synagogues suggests it was an inclusive salary, but, even if so, it is likely that he would have expected and accepted gratuities.

In June 1887, we read that Reverend Applebaum officiated at a special service at the Newcastle Synagogue to celebrate Queen Victoria's Golden Jubilee.[89] Services of this nature were organised at synagogues throughout the British Empire. In Newcastle, Reverend Friedberg, taking as his theme a passage in Leviticus, explained why Jews should rejoice on the occasion. The *Newcastle Daily Chronicle* sent a correspondent, who reported that the worship he observed "was eminently jubilant".[90] Among special features of the service he noted was the singing of the National Anthem in Hebrew. "Taken as a whole the lessons and the singing did credit to Hebrew minstrelsy", he wrote approvingly.

The ostentatious patriotism of the occasion would remain a feature of British Jewish life well into the twentieth century. In pre-Zionist days,

---

88   *JW,* 22nd October 1886, p.6.
89   *JC,* 24th June 1887, p.16
90   *NDC,* 22nd June 1887, p.4.

there was no competing focus of loyalty for British Jews. Full political and legal emancipation in Britain had only recently been achieved. It had opened the door for Jews to citizenship in the most powerful and extensive maritime empire the world had ever seen. Acceptance by the host community was therefore seen as a precious prize by the Jewish establishment. There can be no doubt that most middle-class British-born Jews genuinely felt the patriotic sentiments they evinced at the Jubilee. The attitudes of poor, newly-arrived, Russian Jewish immigrants were inevitably different and transforming these immigrants, as soon as possible, into patriotic, English-speaking, law-abiding Britishers was a concern for the leaders of the Newcastle community, as it was for their equivalents in similar Jewish communities elsewhere in the country.

Jeanette Applebaum was pregnant at the time of the Jubilee celebrations and on 14th September 1887 gave birth to her son Samuel, her seventh child to reach adulthood. The Applebaums' home at the time was 13 Victoria Street. The address was in Newcastle's Jewish quarter, to the extent it had one, about three-quarter's of a mile from the synagogue.

In March 1888, the Newcastle community consecrated a recently-purchased burial ground in Elswick. Reverends Friedberg and Applebaum officiated and a procession was formed which passed around the cemetery grounds.[91] A *Newcastle Daily Chronicle* correspondent attended and reported that that the address given by Reverend Friedberg "was eminently impressive, the historic retrospect of which it consisted being in admirable taste."[92]

---

91   *JC*, 9th March 1888, p.14.
92   *NDC*, 5th March 1888, p.4.

In February 1889, Jeanette gave birth to another son, Mark Applebaum. He was to grow up to be the most musically talented of all her children. He inherited his father's fine voice and using the stage name "Syd Kirby" worked in music hall until his early death in 1923. At the time of his birth, the family were living at 48 Villa Place in Newcastle, about two hundred yards closer to the synagogue than their previous home. The house appears to have been the Applebaum home for the remainder of their time in Newcastle.

The 1891 census provides a snapshot of the circumstances of the Applebaum family at number 48. The census records those present in the property on the night of 5th/6th April 1891. David Applebaum and his wife, whose ages are given as 36 and 37 respectively, lived there with their eight children, none over sixteen. No lodgers or domestic servants are recorded. No occupation is given for their eldest son, Maurice, but he is not stated to be at school. On the face of it, the entire household relied on David Applebaum's earnings. They were however fortunate in having extra space at home. David Applebaum's sister Annie had lived with them from their early days in Newcastle. In December 1890 she married Nathan Bomberg, a Polish-born Jewish draper, and moved out to a marital home about half a mile away. It was one less person for David Applebaum to support, although no doubt Jeanette felt the absence of help with the children and around the home.

Villa Place appears to have been an ethnically mixed street in 1891. The Applebaums had Morris Levi, a tailor and his family, as neighbours on one side and James Sticks, a Scottish widower and his family, on the other. Ten years later, after the Applebaums had gone, the 1901 census shows a street far more Jewish in composition, a consequence of a further decade of Jewish immigration from Russia.

Continuing immigration presented a problem to the synagogue elders in Newcastle. How could they welcome the new immigrants into the congregation and assimilate them into the British Jewish way when their attitudes to religious practice were so alien? British Jewry had evolved practices its leaders considered to be modern, seemly and worthy of respect. Key figures in the development of this *Minhag Anglia*, the English way of worship, were the Chief Rabbis, Nathan Adler and his son and successor, Hermann Adler. The Adlers led mainstream orthodox British Jewry for an astonishing 66 years, from 1845 to 1911. Under their rabbinates, a distinctive form of British Jewish clergyman emerged. Called "ministers" and not "rabbis" and with the title "Reverend", they were required to preach regularly and in English, to wear appropriate clerical garb, so-called "canonicals", to carry out pastoral duties and ensure that worship was properly conducted. Instead of the traditional hum of gossip and sound of scurrying about during services, congregants were to be forbidden to chatter or move seats. Hermann Adler considered this need for decorum so important that he seems to have taken to task the elders of the Newcastle synagogue over this issue, among others, at a meeting with them the day after he attended the consecration of the new synagogue in August 1880.[93]

Many of the new immigrants were uncomfortable with British synagogues and religious practice. The spacious synagogues, with their emphasis on decorous worship and their ministers dressed like Protestant pastors, seemed like churches. There was also the issue of the expense of synagogue membership, very costly to poor, immigrant, manual workers. The response of many of the new Eastern European Jewish immigrants was to form their own independent, small, traditionally-run places of worship. These proliferated in London's East End, but were also present in other cities, notably Leeds.

---

93   *JC*, 27th August 1880, p.7.

The leaders of the Newcastle Jewish community wished both to prevent their growing community fragmenting and welcome the new immigrants. Reverend Friedberg and others rented a house at 12 Villa Place to serve as place of worship for immigrants. Here they could conduct services in their own way and the building could be used as a study hall.[94] Reverend Friedberg left in due course for a post in Liverpool and was replaced in April 1891 by Reverend Mendelsohn BA, formerly of East Melbourne.[95] In May 1891, the *Jewish Chronicle* carried a report announcing that as a result of the increase in the size of the Jewish community in Newcastle an additional place of worship, affiliated to the main Newcastle synagogue and called a *Beth Hamedrash*, had been opened.[96] Donations had been obtained and a suite of rooms had been rented at 225 Westgate Road. There was no suggestion in the news report that the *Beth Hamedrash* was exclusively for the use of recent immigrants. Presumably, the community's representative, who provided the news item to the *Jewish Chronicle*, had no wish to see Newcastle Jewry portrayed as divided. The new place of worship was consecrated by Reverend Mendelsohn. Afternoon prayers were said and Reverend Applebaum, it was reported, then recited Psalm 30, a Psalm of David traditionally intoned on such occasions. It was a crowded service and a festive occasion. Refreshments were served and toasts made, first to the Queen and then to the health of members of the organising committee.

During these years, the *Jewish Chronicle* contains numerous mentions of David Applebaum officiating as reader of the Newcastle synagogue, including in services for the High Holidays, weddings and special

94   Olsover, op. cit., p.37.
95   *JC*, 24th April 1891, p.16.
96   *JC*, 29th May 1891, p.19.

events.[97] Meanwhile his family continued to grow. On 24th August 1891, Jeanette gave birth to another son, Harry, and on 26th April 1893 to a daughter, Rebecca. Both children were born at 48 Villa Place. There were now ten children at home.

97   During the period 1886-94, mentions of David Applebaum's activities in Newcastle in the *Jewish Chronicle* include: 1886: 10th September, p.1; 1887: 24th June, p.16; 23rd September, p.11; 1888: 9th March, p.14; 14th September, p.11; 1889: 1st November, p.1; 1890: 19th September, p.15; 28th September, p.1; 3rd October, p 15; 1891: 29th May, pp.1, 19; 18th December, p.15; 1892: 30th September, p.19; 1893: 8th September, p.17; 15th September, p.17; 22nd September, p.18; 1894: 5th October, p.16; 19th October, p.19.

11. End of an Appointment

In 1894, David Applebaum's work in Newcastle came to an end. Either he was told his contract would not be renewed or he informed the leaders of the community that he wished to move on. What happened is not clear, but inferences may be drawn from news reports and advertisements in the Jewish press. Other sources of information are the Newcastle synagogue's cash book and ledger, which survive from April 1892 and November 1894, respectively.

In March and April 1894, the synagogue advertised for a replacement for Reverend Mendelsohn, who was leaving after three years to become minister in Bristol. His replacement was Reverend Morris Rosenbaum, who was appointed minister and head school master in June 1894.[98] Then, in August, advertisements were placed on behalf of the Hebrew Congregation, Newcastle on Tyne, in identical terms for two weeks in the *Jewish Chronicle* and, in August and September, in *eight* successive weeks of the *Jewish World*, as follows:

> *Wanted by the above Congregation, gentleman to act as mohel, shochet & hazan at a salary of £2 -10s [i.e. £2.50p] per week and perquisites. Applicants not to be over 35 years of age and must be certified by the Chief Rabbi. Expenses will be paid for the successful candidate only. Applications to be sent to ....."*

No start date was specified, but, as brief mentions in the *Jewish Chronicle* attest, David Applebaum continued in post and officiated as reader during the festivals of *Rosh Hashonah, Yom Kippur and Succos*. In November, Reverend Israel Yelin of Manchester was appointed his

---

98   JC, 16th March 1894, p.3; JW, 6th April 1894, p.1; JC, 8th June 1894, p.19; JW, 8th
      June 1894, p.7.

successor.[99] Reverend Applebaum's last weekly salary payment of £2 10s was made on 16th December 1894 and Reverend Yelin's first, for the same amount, on 22nd December 1894. As promised in the synagogue's advertisement, Reverend Yelin also received five guineas [£5. 25p] for his expenses.

The synagogue's books of account record some large sums paid to or for the benefit of Reverend Applebaum in 1894. On 6th December, £10 was paid and on 12th December a further £54, both described as "on a/c of grant". On 21st December, £40 was "deposited at Cook's Bank for Applebaum". Some small payments are also recorded as having been received from Reverend Applebaum. These are described as "repayments": 15s [75p] on 6th December, 9s 9d [49p] on 14th February 1895 and £5 1s 10p [£5.09p] on 1st August 1895. There is no record of any further repayments by him. It seems that as his employment with the synagogue was coming to an end in 1894, he received some substantial sums in addition to his salary. The status and purpose of these amounts is not clear. "Grant" suggests payments which are non-repayable. The "repayments" must relate to other matters.

One interpretation is that it was the synagogue that decided either not to renew or to terminate David Applebaum's contract. He had served the *shul* for eight years and the congregation was used to a fairly rapid turnover in clergymen. The grants paid to him may have originated from a wish not to cast a clergyman with a large family into destitution. There does not seem to have been any *other* recognition of his service to the community. Reverend Pearlson, reader for seven years until 1882, was

99   *JC*, 16th November 1894, p.21. In succeeding years, the new *chazan*'s surname was sometimes times spelled "Yellin" by the press and sometimes "Yelin". The latter appears to have been his preference, which is adopted here for the sake of consistency.

presented with "a purse of money" on his resignation, Reverend Friedberg in 1891, after five years as minister, received a "massive gold watch" and his successor, Reverend Mendelsohn in 1894, after three years, received "an illuminated address, set of bronzes, marble timepiece and a cheque".[100] Reverend Applebaum does not appear to have been presented with anything. Perhaps it was felt that he had received recognition enough for his services through the financial grants he had been paid. In any event, the grants he received were not enough to tide him over until he found a new appointment. According to the synagogue's ledger, he borrowed a further £5 in February 1895, which he re-paid, together with a shilling's interest, six months later.

But perhaps he wanted to go. Reverend Applebaum's salary was £130 a year. Looking at job advertisements for *chazanim* in the Jewish press, a salary of £130 was on the low side for a significant provincial congregation, perhaps a reflection of the Newcastle synagogue's strained financial circumstances.[101] At one end of the scale, in Bristol, the combined post of *shochet*, second reader and *mohel* was advertised at £77 15s p.a; not quite the same as Reverend Applebaum's job because the duties of a second reader were probably quite light.[102] The Leeds Great Synagogue, an employer comparable to Newcastle, advertised for a *chazan* and choirmaster at £3 a week, which was ten shillings [50p] a week more than Newcastle, and without having to perform the

100 JC, 8th December 1882, p.4; JC, 22nd May 1891, p.9; JC, 6th April 1894, p.23.
101 By 1900, the Newcastle community had increased the salary of its *chazen/shochet/mohel* from £130 p.a. to £182 p.a. and reduced his cantorial duties by appointing a second reader (job advertisement, JW, 9th March 1900, p.379). However, five years later, the salary was put back to £156 p.a. and the qualification "must be able to read music" was added (job advertisement, JW, 13th January 1905, p.311).
102 JC, 20th April 1894, p.3; JW 11th May 1894, p.1; JW 18th May 1894 p.1. The base salary was £70 p.a., plus £7.15s p.a. from a bequest.

additional duties of *shochet* and *mohel*.[103] At the other end of the scale, the New West End Synagogue in Bayswater, London, whose beautiful building was a citadel of anglicised Jewry, advertised for a reader and secretary, the latter duties being nominal initially and there being no requirement to act as *shochet* and *mohel*, on a three-year contract at £300 p.a..[104] Of course, Reverend Applebaum's Newcastle salary was not one to be given up lightly, especially by a clergyman whose family was large and whose standard of English and probable lack of a secular education put fashionable West End New synagogues out of his league. Nevertheless, there may have been good reasons for his leaving Newcastle, both personal and financial.

By 1894, the Applebaums had seven sons, three of whom had attained their *barmitzvah,* and there may have been a desire to move the family to a location which would give the boys greater and more varied possibilities in life. There was also a wish not to lose contact with a friend and relative. For most of his life, David Applebaum's closest friend was another Dobriner, Morris Grey, originally Mauritz Grauer. They had been boys together in Dobrin, David being senior to Morris by a couple of years. Morris Grey's grandson, Ronald Shenker, believed that the two may have been first cousins, David's mother being sister to Morris Grey's father, although Brian Appleby, Maurice Applebaum's grandson, had never heard any such story.[105] Morris Grey seems to have followed

---

103 *JC*, 23rd November 1894, p.22.
104 *JC*, 1st March 1895, p.17.
105 Conversations with Ronald Shenker, 17th January 1989 and 19th January 1989; conversation with Brian Appleby, 4th December 2011. For the sake of consistency, the anglicised form of the family surname is spelled "Grey" in this account, although during this period the family seem to have varied the spelling between "Grey" and "Gray" almost indiscriminately. For example, in Rebecca Grey's 1899 marriage certificate she is "Gray" but in the English abstract of her contemporaneous *katuva* (Jewish marriage contract), she is "Grey"!

the Applebaums to Newcastle in the late 1880s.[106] He brought with him a wife and three daughters. Ronald Shenker believed that Morris Grey worked as *chazan* in the North-East, but no evidence to establish this has yet been found. In the 1891 census, the Greys are recorded as living 25 John Street, Newcastle, and Morris Grey's occupation is given as "Travelling Jeweller". In any event, by 1894 Morris Grey had secured an appointment as a *chazan* in London and his departure and a wish to remain in contact with the Greys would have been a factor in any decision that David Applebaum's took about his own future and that of his own family.

Financially speaking, a move by the family to London offered the possibility of David Applebaum not only finding a post as reader on better pay but also, if the employing synagogue permitted it, of working as a *mohel* on a freelance basis. In the fourteen or so years since the Applebaums had left Wilkes Street, the Jewish population of London had doubled. There would be many more opportunities to provide services as a *mohel* in a great metropolis whose Jewish population was fifty times larger than that of the Newcastle community. In Newcastle, he worked only occasionally as a *mohel* . Taking into account population size, birth rate and infant mortality rate, a rough guess at the number of circumcisions he performed in 1894 is 30-35. If he ever kept a *milah* register, that is, record of circumcisions for the Newcastle community, it has not survived. To get some perspective, however, we can look at circumcisions in Newcastle's sister community in Sunderland. The *milah*

---

106 Morris Grey's youngest daughter, Annie, was born in Poland in about 1885, according to later census returns. David Applebaum's daughter of the same first name was born in Germany at about the same time. If Morris arrived in Newcastle before David, it could only have been by a few months. It is more likely, however, that it was the other way around, with Morris following David once David had found a secure appointment as reader at a local synagogue.

register for Sunderland for 1880-88 is available.[107] For the last complete calendar year, 1887, when the Sunderland community was about two-thirds of the size of Newcastle, the register records 13 circumcisions. A 30- 35 range for Newcastle seven years later, when the population of both communities had increased by further immigration, is therefore probably about right.

If being a *mohel* in Newcastle involved carrying out a *bris* once a week, at most, in London there were *mohelim* who were far more active and a few for whom it was their principal occupation. The economic basis of their activities is, however, unclear because the market for the service was not transparent. Some *mohelim* were members of the Initiation Society, a communal body which both acted as a charity assisting poor families in connection with circumcision and published a list of authorised *mohelim* whom it encouraged the Jewish public to use. These operators were not permitted to advertise nor were they supposed to charge a fee, although they could receive a "donation" in lieu of the time and trouble they expended. Many *mohelim* were not members of the society and one reason for this was in order to be more straightforwardly commercial and to publicise their services. Two non-member *mohelim* who regularly advertised in the Jewish press in the 1890s were Reverend A Tertis and Walter L Phillips, but neither quoted their prices in advertisements.

So what did London *mohelim* actually charge? Some insight is provided by a letter to the *Jewish Chronicle* in 1903[108] in which an indignant correspondent relates that an unnamed, medically-qualified Initiation Society *mohel* had quoted him five guineas (£5.25p) for a *bris*, when the most the correspondent was prepared to pay was a guinea (£1.05p).

---

107   Deposited with Tyne & Wear Archives.
108   *JC*, 16th January 1903, p.9.

This suggests that a guinea may have been the going rate charged to a middle class family. Few Jewish manual workers could afford a guinea a *bris;* it was more than a week's earnings for many of them. At this level, *mohelim* probably charged what the family could afford. Evidence from a 1903 coroner's inquest suggests that this could be as little as 2s 6d (£0.12.5p),[109] although such a fee seems remarkably low for a *mohel*'s time given that a *mohel* was expected to make at least one preliminary visit to a family before a *bris* and one follow-up visit to check on a child's progress after the operation.

Presumably, whether a London *mohel* was generally practising at the top end rather than the bottom of this wide fee range would depend on whether he practised more in the West End and suburbs, and to the middle class, than to poor East Enders. It is easy to see though how David Applebaum might believe that, with a reasonable throughput of circumcisions in a practice aiming to be as upscale as possible, he could earn more as a *mohel* in London than the £2.10s a week he was getting as a composite *chazan/shochet/mohel* in Newcastle. It made sense, though, to seek a synagogue appointment, provided it was one in which he would be permitted to practise fully as a *mohel* on the side. A job as a *chazan* would provide a regular income and a degree of financial security. It would enable him to be seen and known and it would entitle him to call himself "Reverend", which would enhance his professional status. And of course, for a man renowned for his voice and with a love of music, it would give him the opportunity to perform.

While continuing to base himself in the North-East, David Applebaum seems to have spent over a year trying to find a new long-term appointment as a *chazan*. In the meantime, his former job in Newcastle now being filled by Reverend Yelin, he forged a connection with a Jewish community in Sunderland.

---

109 *JW*, 9th January 1903, pp.288-9

12. Sunderland

It is at this point that the narrative of David Applebaum's life intersects one of the most remarkable stories in history of nineteenth-century Jewish immigration into Britain; the migration to Sunderland of a substantial part of the Jewish population of the Russian Lithuanian town of Krottingen.

Sunderland is ten miles south-east of Newcastle. In late Victorian times, Sunderland was a coal port and a shipbuilding town. Its population in 1900 was 146,000, about two-thirds that of Newcastle. Sunderland was the first town in the North-East in modern times to attract Jewish settlement. From the early eighteenth century it received Jews from Germany, the Netherlands and Poland. By 1858, its Jewish population had reached 250 and in 1862 a new synagogue for the community was opened in Moor Street by the Chief Rabbi. By 1876 its Jewish population had risen to about 600.[110] In terms of size of Jewish population, Sunderland was second to Newcastle in the North-East.

From the 1870s, a new stream of Jewish settlers started to reach Sunderland, emanating from Lithuania and in particular from the town of Krottingen (modern Kretinga). It was a border town, of no great size, three miles from the German frontier. How it came to be the main source of immigrants for Sunderland is a classic example of chain migration, that is, the social phenomenon of migrants learning of opportunities and having travel, accommodation and initial employment arranged through family or other relationships with migrants already settled at their destination. In weighing "pull" factors as between one potential destination and another, chain migrators will give more weight than other migrators to the certainty of knowing they will be able to receive assistance at their destination. A non-chain migrator, by contrast, might be more concerned about the underlying economic opportunities that exist at a potential destination.

---

110   Olsover, op.cit., p.266

In 1859, Barnett Bernstein Gillis, a Lithuanian Jew from Krottingen, who had been conscripted into the Russian military, deserted. He was smuggled by friends across the border into Germany and embarked on a timber ship from Memel to Hartlepool. On arrival, he looked for employment and walked to Sunderland, where he found work as a carpenter and glazier. In time, he became a prosperous furniture manufacturer. News of his success reached Krottingen and he was later joined in Sunderland by relatives and other people from his home town.[111] In 1889, a disastrous fire destroyed the synagogue, chedar, rabbinical buildings and much of the timber-built Jewish quarter in Krottingen. Funds were raised in Sunderland to assist. As a result of the fire and the existence of the Sunderland connection, the flow of emigrants from Krottingen increased. By the early 1890s there were about 1000 Jews in Sunderland and over half of these were connected with Krottingen.[112]

The Jewish community in Sunderland was far more divided than that of Newcastle. The Lithuanian immigrants included learned and religious leaders of the Krottingen community. They were unimpressed with the piety and practices of the anglicised Jews in the Sunderland community, were devoted to religious study, and were not prepared to accept the authority of the Chief Rabbi in religious matters on which they disagreed. A split in the Sunderland community was inevitable.[113]

The Lithuanian Jews decided to set up a house of worship on traditional orthodox lines, which would be separate but not wholly independent

111 Gordon Leigh, *From Kretinga to Sunderland; A Jewish Chain Migration from Lithuania - Cause and Effect 1850-1930s* M.A. thesis, University of Newcastle – Department of History, 2002, pp. 20A-22 (Tyne & Wear Archives).

112 Jon Seligman, Sunderland – *A Litvak Community in North East England*, www.seligman.org.il/sunderland_jews.html (accessed 6th August 2012).

113 Arnold Levy, *History of the Sunderland Jewish Community 1755-1955*, Macdonald, London, 1956, pp.159-162.

from the Sunderland congregation. Called initially a *Chevrah Torah* (society for the study of the Torah) and later a *Beth Hamedrash*, it was first established in Zion Street. The premises soon became too small for the numbers who wished to worship there and in December 1894 a former Quaker Meeting House in Villiers Street North was rented.[114] Its opening was reported by the *Jewish Chronicle:*

> *"In connection with the Chevrah Torah, a new place of worship was formally opened in Villiers Street on Sunday last. The Rev Mr Applebaum read the usual afternoon service, which was followed by the recital of Psalm XXX. After reading the prayer for the Queen and the Royal Family, the Rev J Phillips* [Minister of the Moor Street Synagogue] *delivered an address. He complained of the dissensions in many chevras* [religious societies], *advised them to assimilate themselves to and imitate their neighbours in language and dress and impressed upon them the duty of carefully observing the laws of the country, and living in amity, concord and peace".*[115]

The inauguration concluded with the usual refreshments and toasts, but may have been less than a fully joyous occasion. Reverend Phillips' address reads like an admonishment of the *Litvak* (Lithuanian) migrants for wanting to worship separately and to cling to old ways. The anglicised, mostly middle class Jews of Sunderland had come to find that they were now sharing the town with a re-constituted East European *shtetl* , cast up on the Durham coast, and their feelings about this were ambivalent. Their *Litvak* co-religionists, meanwhile, regarded them as *Englishe Chayer* ("pompous would-be English gentlemen", Yiddish).[116] It was not, however, for another five years that the split from the rest of the Sunderland community would become complete.

---

114   Levy, ibid·
115   *JC*, 4th January 1895, p.20.
116   Leigh, op. cit., p.4. The expression might be more robustly translated as "English rubbish" or even "English animals".

David Applebaum is reported again in connection with the *Chevrah Torah* in Sunderland in April 1895 when he officiated as *chazan* during the Passover services and was presented with a "handsome marble clock".[117] The minutes of the *Chevrah Torah* have disappeared and it is not clear whether he merely travelled to Sunderland to officiate on significant occasions for a one-off fee or whether he was there each Saturday acting as *chazan* on a continuing basis. The latter is possible, but it would have entailed him having to stay over in Sunderland each Friday night as to travel by public transport to and from Sunderland between sunset on Friday evening and sunset on Saturday evening would have been a desecration of the Sabbath.

Clearly, the immigrants from Krottingen appreciated his trips to Sunderland. He was still very much an East European Jew in manner and habits, and may have been regarded as a kindred spirit, although his dialect of Yiddish was different from theirs. It is odd, though, that his connection with them does not seem to have softened the Applebaum family's view of Lithuanian Jews, often stereotyped by Polish Jews as being unemotional, pedantic and hyper- critical. Jeanette Applebaum's standing advice to her children in later years, given perhaps only half seriously, was "never marry a *Litvak*".

117 *JC*, 19th April 1895, p.18.

On 17th May 1895[118] and again a week later, an advertisement appeared in the *Jewish Chronicle* as follows:

"Chevra Bikkur Cholim [in Hebrew script, "Society for Visiting the Sick"]

Fashion Street Synagogue: Wanted for the above Synagogue, a Chazen and Baal- Korah ["skilled Torah reader"]. *Applications in writing with credentials from the Chief Rabbi to be made on or before 28th inst to...."*

David Applebaum applied, got the job, and in August it was announced that he had been elected reader and *Baal-Korah* of the Fashion Street *shul*.[119] Getting the job meant attending an initial interview and audition and there was no mention in the advertisement of the expenses of a successful candidate being paid. It was a step down by comparison with his appointment in Newcastle. Fashion Street was less than 300 yards from the Applebaums' old East End home in Wilkes Street. Its name had been given ironically by some "dead and gone wag", suggested Israel Zangwill in *The Children of the Ghetto*. "It is a dull, squalid, narrow, thoroughfare in the East End of London", he wrote, "connecting Spitalfields with Whitechapel and branching off in blind alleys".[120] The congregation, according to the Jewish Year Book 1896/7 was small, only 54 members. The synagogue's advertisement does not mention pay, but it would have been less that Newcastle. A nearby East End *shul*, Old Castle Street, also advertised for a *chazan* and *Baal Korah* in the summer of 1895 and included salary details; only £75 p.a.[121] Fashion Street was probably paying about the same. Still, taking up the job must have made

118   JC, 17th May 1895, p.3; 24th May 1895, p.22.
119   JC, 30th August 1895, p.11.
120   Zangwill, op.cit., p.9.
121   JC, 19th July 1895, p. 19.

economic sense. As the Fashion Street congregation did not require its new *chazan* also to act as *shochet* and *mohel,* there was scope for David Applebaum to increase his total earnings beyond his Newcastle salary by taking on freelance work. Getting the job must have been a huge relief for the family. There can be no doubt that in 1895 the family was under considerable financial pressure.

We do not know when David Applebaum started his new job, but we can take a reasonable guess at when Jeanette and her children moved down to London. On his election as *chazan,* Jeanette was almost seven months pregnant. The child, named Manny (Manassah), was born on 7th November 1895 and was to be Jeanette's eleventh child to reach adulthood. He was born in Newcastle[122] and Jeanette and her children must have moved to London as soon as she was well enough to make the long train journey south. The child's name would certainly have been chosen to honour David's father, but it may also have been selected on an epithetic basis because it was felt that the family was experiencing a time of crisis. After the move, it was remembered that the child's birth had not been registered and, on 6th January 1896, this was undertaken at the Whitechapel Register Office. The baby's place of birth was falsely stated to be the family's new London address. To register a false address for place of birth was an offence, but the Applebaums were not prepared to make an expensive train journey back to Newcastle merely to register the birth at the Newcastle Register Office, which was the appropriate registry for the Westgate Sub-District in which Villa Place was located.

---

122 Manny Appleby, the author's father, maintained all his life that he was told he was born in Newcastle. This is also what he told the British army when he joined up during the First World War, as the record of his army medical examination on 14th May 1917 attests (accessible via www.ancestry.co.uk/ among "British Army WWI Pensions Records 1914-20", last accessed 16th August 2012).

David Applebaum may have initially gone down to London on his own, leaving his family to follow. If this is what happened, his eldest son, Maurice, then about twenty years-old, would have taken charge of moving his mother and brothers and sisters. Their new home was at 75 Whitechapel Road, on the north side of the wide and busy street. The building has long since been demolished and is now (2012) a bank with offices above. The accommodation David Applebaum rented is likely to have comprised no more than four or five rooms located above a shop. At the time of the 1891 census the shop had been a clothes shop and there had been six people living in the rooms above it. Now, after the Applebaums had moved in, thirteen adults and children were crammed into the same space. The number of occupants was increased on 6th August 1897 by the birth of the Applebaums' twelfth and last child to reach adulthood, Lazarus, who came to be called Leonard.

14. An East End *Chazan*

David Applebaum spent his last eleven years of life living and working in the East End. The reason he stayed there was because he made his living in providing services to Jewish people and the East End was where the Jews were. Of the 135,000 Jews living in London at the end of the nineteenth century, 120,000 were clustered in the East End.[123] It was not a ghetto in the sense that concentrated Jewish settlement there was the result of compulsion, although it was often referred to as a ghetto by many contemporaries. As regards ethnic homogeneity and difference from the host community, London's burgeoning Jewish quarter had no peer in the metropolis. To gentile visitors, even sympathetic ones, it seemed like an exotic, alien city within the city.

The East End contained a myriad of synagogues, some scarcely a few yards from each other. The anglicised Jewish elite, based in the West End or in the suburbs, referred to all of these East End houses of worship as *chevrot* (plural of *chevra,* a club or society), as if they were all the same, but they were far from uniform either in size or type. They ranged from humble one-room conventicles, in one reported instance, in

---

123   Alderman, op.cit., p.12.

77

someone's kitchen,[124] to synagogues with several hundred subscribing members. Many of the synagogues owed their foundation to the wish of immigrants to worship with fellow countrymen. There was a Grodno *shul*, a Kovno *shul*, a Warsaw *shul*, a Konin *shul* and a Petrikoff *shul*.[125] Many of the smaller establishments were dirty and dilapidated, but to poor manual workers, they offered the possibility of performing their collective devotions at little expense. The *Chevra Kehol Chassidim* in Fieldgate Street in the East End had 52 members and levied five pence [£0.02p] a week in membership dues.[126] By contrast, the Great

---

124 "A Humble Chevra Room" by "A Visitor Among the Poor" (JC, 23rd August 1895, p.13). The visitor went to visit a sick woman in Hanbury Street. The following is a short extract from a lengthy article:
I made my way up a pair of rather steep and winding stairs which led into a room. Let me try to describe the room. It was rather large for the neighbourhood and was a sort of kitchen. It had an ample fireplace the top of which formed an open recess in which a number of all sorts of objects could be stowed away. By the side of the fireplace was a kitchen dresser with its ordinary supply of cups and saucers and crockery. A long table and forms made of the roughest deal and put together in an amateurish, not to say clumsy way, formed the other items of furniture. The room led into a bedroom and there were large windows in the partitioning wall so that they could see into the bedroom even when the door was shut, quite easily. Another flight of stairs led from the room to the apartments above.

The woman I had come to see had had an accident. She had fallen down the stairs which led into the street and was lying in bed in the large kitchen I have described. Well, there was nothing remarkable in all this, your readers will think. But what will they say when I tell them that behind her bed was a fairly large Aron Hakodesh or Ark and by the side of it a Reader's desk? Such, however is the fact. The room was not only a kitchen and a bedroom, it was also a shul or rather a chevra.

It seems that a dozen or so of poor foreigners have clubbed together to form a minyan. They subscribe twopence a week and pay the occupier of the house in Hanbury Street where I was visiting two shillings a week for the use of the kitchen as a Shul.

125 Geoffrey Alderman, The Federation of Synagogues 1887-1987, Federation of Synagogues, London, 1987, p.11.

126 Alderman, ibid., p.12.

78

Synagogue in Duke Street, required £3.10s [£3.50p] a year.[127] Anglicised West Enders regarded the *chevrot* with mixed feelings. There was a recognition that the East End synagogues were vestiges of an old world closer to their religion's ancient roots. However, the religious practices of the *chevrot*, the passions expressed and the length, noise and frequency of services, seemed to many of the anglicised Jewish middle class un-evolved, unnecessary and at times embarrassing.

It was beyond the means of the smallest synagogues to employ a *chazan*; his function would be performed by a member of the congregation. In larger congregations, a reader could be afforded, but at low rates. It was not only demand which depressed the pay rates for *chazanim*, it was also supply. Despite the low opinion which traditionalist East European Jews held of the piety of British Jewry, a view which many continued to hold long after they had migrated to Britain, there never seems to have been any shortage of gentlemen from the Continent available to come to Britain to serve as *chazanim*.

Another factor keeping David Applebaum in the East End and preventing him finding a position with a wealthy and well-paying congregation in the West End or suburbs may have been insufficient fluency in English. A *chazan* was not expected to preach, let alone preach in English, but *shul* business in any synagogue of size was conducted in English and there were increasing numbers of second generation congregants whose knowledge of Yiddish might be poor. A weak knowledge of spoken and written English would also prevent a *chazan* assisting in other duties at a synagogue, such as acting as secretary or in teaching in any associated Jewish school.

---

127   Eugene C. Black, *The Social Politics of Anglo-Jewry 1880-1920*, Basil Blackwell, Oxford, 1988, p.60.

The main organisation of orthodox British synagogues in the late nineteenth century, then as now, was the United Synagogue movement. Brought together by Chief Rabbi Nathan Adler in the 1860s and with its charitable status established by the United Synagogue Act of 1870, it represented the anglicised, modernising mainstream. The small East End *chevrot* were outside its sphere. It was the rich, orthodox Jewish MP for Whitechapel, Sir Samuel Montagu, who, in 1887, was instrumental in corralling many of the *chevrot* into a new grouping, the Federation of Minor Synagogues ("Minor" being dropped from the title after a couple of years). The Federation remained under the general authority of the Chief Rabbi and his *Beth Din* (religious court), but the intention was that it would be more devout and traditionalist than the United Synagogue. Mixed sex choirs, for example, were opposed. By 1903, some 39 synagogues had become federated, with their burial and benefit societies amalgamated, in order to provide more efficient administration and achieve economies of scale. However, despite its cultural conservatism, all administrative activities and internal meetings of the Federation were conducted in English.[128]

A *chazan* who served a provincial synagogue as reader, *shochet* and *mohel* may not have been deeply learned, but possessed a combination of practical skills and religious knowledge that made him invaluable to the community. For this reason, in Newcastle, the minister and the *chazan/shochet/mohel* were paid the same basic salary of £ 130 p.a. But did a *chazan* deserve the same degree of respect and deference? In this regard, David Applebaum's move back to London in 1895 coincided with a flurry of comment in the *Jewish Chronicle* on whether a *chazan* should properly be referred to as "Reverend", as ministers were.

---

128   Gartner, op.cit., pp.203-6; Black, op.cit., pp.60-66

The one-sided discussion of the issue cannot be described as a debate; there was no one speaking up for *chazanim*. But then no one seemed to think they were doing their job badly. The root of the matter lay in a deficiency in the communal status of late nineteenth-century British synagogue ministers. This was a consequence of their training and the conception of their role.

Jews College, a British seminary for the training of synagogue ministers, was set up in 1855. The intention was to develop a corps of Jewish clergymen who could officiate in synagogues, preach in English to an expanding and increasingly anglicised Jewish population and represent with dignity the Jewish faith to the Christian world. Their training did not involve deep and ancient erudition. Instead, there was an intention that students combine Jewish religious studies with modern university studies to degree level. The products of Jews College were to be called "Reverend". The Chief Rabbi had the power to ordain successful students and grant the title "Rabbi", but he did not do so. He was a Chief Rabbi with no rabbis under him; a chief with no indians.

The complaint about *chazanim* being called "Reverend" emanated originally from Charles Samuel the benefactor of Jews College, who at an annual meeting of the College in 1895, raised the issue of restricting the use of the title. A letter to the *Jewish Chronicle* from an anonymous correspondent, presumably linked in some way with Jews College, railed against the unfairness "to those who have studied much …[for the title to be used]…by anyone whose only qualification is a fine voice".[129] There were subsequent letters: "It is monstrous that the most obscure Chazan or Shochet should as a matter of course prefix to his patronymic the title named, don a clerical get-up and pass as a 'Jewish Minister'", wrote

---

129   *JC*, 10th May 1895, p.8.

a further anonymous correspondent.[130] Another called for the ending not only of the use of the title "Reverend" by *chazanim* but also their wearing of "clerical garb".[131]

In due course, the *Jewish Chronicle* took up the issue with a learned editorial.[132] It was "most undesirable that unqualified men should pose as members of the clergy", the paper asserted. In England, "a habit has grown up of prefixing the title Reverend without the slightest discrimination to all who are concerned, however remotely, in the religious work of the synagogue". The conclusion of the editorial was that ways needed to be found to upgrade the status of ministers to set them above others participating in communal life. And this is what eventually occurred.

In 1903, agreement was reached for the Chief Rabbi to certify as "Rabbi" those Jews College students who had completed appropriate training and examinations. This development was paralleled by an increase in the element of traditional study in training in Jews College. It was not, however, until after 1908 that successful Jews College students started to be called "Rabbi" and not until after the First World War that Jews College was graduating rabbis with a mastery of the Talmud.[133]

David Applebaum was no doubt aware of the criticism being levelled at *chazanim*, even if he was unlikely to have toiled his way through the *Jewish Chronicle's* lengthy editorial. He continued until his death

---

130 *JC*, 24th May 1895, p.7

131 *JC*, 14th June 1895, p.11.

132 *JC*, 14th June 1895, pp.15-6.

133 Black, op.cit., pp.52-3; Endelman, op.cit., pp.13, 119; Raymond Apple, *Herman Gollancz & the title of rabbi in British Jewry*, presentation to Jewish Historical Society of England Israel Branch, 30th May 2010, www.oztorah.com/2010/06/hermann-gollancz-the-title-of-rabbi-in-british-jewry/ (accessed 9th March 2012).

to use the title "Reverend" and it remained the practice among British synagogues that employed professional *chazanim* to afford them this title. Although controversy over the use of the title for *chazanim* rumbled on in British Jewry for decades, its continuing use reflected a degree of communal respect for the role performed by the *chazan* of a synagogue and the men who undertook it, notwithstanding their educational shortcomings.

15. The Synagogue of Fashion Street

David Applebaum started work at the *Chevra Bikkur Cholim* Fashion Street Synagogue in about December 1895. He worked for the *shul* for just over two years and there are no mentions of him in the Jewish press during this period.

Writing an individual history of many of the East End's small synagogues is a difficult task. Records have usually not survived. The same congregations may be known by two or three different names. They also tended to form, amalgamate, split up or relocate, whether for practical, personal or religious reasons, just as often as their congregants saw fit. These factors have led to problems in identification and the name "Fashion Street Synagogue" is an eminent example of this difficulty. The JewishGen JCR-UK website "Synagogues in the East End and City of London according to Name of Street in which they are, or were, situated",[134] lists seven names for congregations which contain the words "Fashion Street", as follows:

1. "Fashion Court, E1 – Fashion Street Chevra"
2. "Fashion Street (New Court) E1 – Mikvah Synagogue"
3. "Fashion Street, E1 – Mikrah Chevrah"
4. "Fashion Street, E1 – Fashion Street Sphardish Synagogue"
5. "Fashion Street, E1 – United Friends Synagogue"
6. "16 Fashion Street, E1 – Fashion Street Synagogue "
7. "45 Fashion Street, E1 – Yanover Synagogue"

Further synagogues in Fashion Street are mentioned by other sources,[135] including:

8. The "Bessarabia Kiev Synagogue" and
9. The "*Sphardish* Synagogue".

---

134 *Jewish Congregations of the City of London and the East End of London*, www. jewishgen.org/jcr-uk/london/East_End_London.htm (accessed 10th August 2012).
135 See below.

Some of these names are just different names for the same congregation, but disentangling the names is far from straightforward and one sympathises with the decision of the compilers of the JewishGen website to provide as comprehensive a list as possible of all known names and leave it at that.

During the period in which David Applebaum worked in Fashion Street, there were always two congregations in the street. One was David Applebaum's employer, the *Chevra Bikkur Cholim*, and the other was a slightly larger synagogue, the *Chevra Mikra* (loosely, "Society of the Bible"). The name of the latter was sometimes misspelt as "Chevra Mikvah", both in the Jewish press[136] and in the records of the Federation of Synagogues.[137] Both of these congregations were early members of the Federation. Representatives of the *Chevra Bikkur Cholim* were present at the Federation's first meeting on 4th December 1887. Representatives of the *Chevra Mikra* may have attended also, perhaps in an unofficial capacity, but were certainly present at the Federation's second meeting on 6th January 1888.[138] The *Chevra Mikra* went on to merge with the Princelet Street Synagogue in January 1898.[139] The *Bikkur Cholim* continued its independent existence for a little longer, amalgamating with the Fieldgate Street Synagogue in May 1899.[140]

---

136 e.g. *JC*, 15th April 1898, p.32.
137 e.g. Minute of Federation board meeting , 17th February 1889, LMA ACC 2893/001.
138 The Federation's record of its second meeting on 6th January 1888 states that *Chevra Mikra* was one of the synagogues that had joined the Federation since the previous meeting. However, the record of the Federation's 4th December 1887 meeting indicates that "Fashion Court" representatives had attended. Perhaps they were present at the earlier meeting on an informal basis (LMA ACC 2893/001).
139 Melnick, op. cit, pp.83-4.
140 Federation board meeting, 28th May 1899, LMA ACC/2893/001.

Synagogues came and went in the narrow, two-hundred-yard-long street and it is frequently unclear to which congregation a contemporary reference to "Fashion Street Synagogue" relates. In February 1899, a congregation called "the Bessarabia Kiev Synagogue", located in Fashion Street, joined the Federation.[141] Its name suggests that its congregants originated from what would then be termed South Russia, but would be Moldova and Ukraine today. The congregation may have been utilising premises previously occupied by the *Chevra Mikra*. In March 1903, the Yanover Synagogue, based at 44 Finch Street, joined the Federation, but by February 1904 seems to have relocated to 45 Fashion Street. Within a year, it had amalgamated with the Wilkes Street Synagogue.[142] The board minutes of the Federation report the admission of yet another "Fashion Street Synagogue" in December 1905.[143] The congregation was based at No 45, which indicates that it may have taken over premises previously occupied by the Yanover Synagogue. By 1905, there was also a *chevra* in Fashion Street known as the *Sphardish* or *Swardish* Synagogue.[144] This congregation moved in 1911 from Fashion Street to new premises in a former school building in Philpot Street[145] and then became the Philpot Street Sphardish Synagogue. The synagogue's name originated from its mode of worship, which derived from the *Nusach Sefard* rite of the

---

141   Federation board meeting, 12th February 1899, LMA ACC/2893/001. The name of the *chevra* was later shortened to "*Kiever* Synagogue".

142   Federation board meeting, 10th March 1903, LMA ACC/2803/001; *JC*, 13th March 1903, p.25; Federation board meetings 1st February 1904, 8th May 1905, both LMA ACC/2893/002. The *Jewish Chronicle* gives a Finch Street rather than Fashion Street address for the Yanover Synagogue at the time of its merger with the Wilkes Street Synagogue (*JC*, 12th May 1905, p.19). There are several candidates for the town in Eastern Europe from which the congregation's founders originated.

143   Federation board meeting, 18th December 1905, LMA ACC/2893/002; *JW*, 22nd December 1905, p.321.

144   *JC*, 13th January 1905, p.3; Federation board meeting 8th May 1905, LMA ACC/2893/002.

145   *JC*, 6th January 1911, p.28.

Chassidim, a prayer liturgy, existing in various versions, which modified Ashkenazi liturgy by incorporating Sephardi elements.[146]

The Yiddish-speaking congregants of these *chevrot* would have referred to their synagogues by a Hebrew or Yiddish name and would not have been confused, as we are, when a street name is used as primary identifier. Congregants would also have been well aware of the liturgical differences which existed between these small synagogues, which did not adhere to a single, invariable, ancient religious rite. Some of these differences could be quite minor. Others could be significant and might isolate a *chevra* from its neighbours. In the former category was the practice of the *Chevra Mikra* to make a special celebration each year on the traditional birth/death date of the law-giver, Moses. On the merger of the synagogue with the Princelet Street Synagogue, it seems to have been easily agreed that this practice would be maintained by the merged congregation.[147] In the latter category were the practices of the Fashion Street Sphardish synagogue. This *chevra* pursued a fervent and intense Chassidic form of worship which was unusual in the East End at the time and which made it difficult for contemporaries to envisage the *shul* merging with any other local synagogue.[148]

146   Ibid; *The Jewish History Channel: The Difference Between The Sephardic Nusach (rite) and "Nusach Sefard"*, 5th February 2009, in blog of Joels W Davidi, http://ha-historion.blogspot.co.uk/2009/02/ difference-between-sephardim-and-nusach… (accessed, 1st September 2012).

147   Melnick, op.cit, p.84.

148   *JC*, 6th January 1911, p.28.

16. Great Alie Street Synagogue

In December 1897, the Great Alie Street synagogue advertised for a *chazan* and *baal korah*.[149] David Applebaum applied. His efforts were successful and on 27th March 1898, he was elected reader of the Great Alie Street Synagogue "by a large majority".[150] He may not have started work immediately and there is a news report in the *Jewish Chronicle*, contradicted by the *Jewish World*, which indicates that he officiated at the April 1898 Passover services at Princelet Street Synagogue.[151] However, he was certainly in post by *Rosh Hashonah* and *Yom Kippur*, when he officiated at the Great Alie Street Synagogue for the High Holidays.[152] The amount of his salary in his new job is not known, but all the evidence points to the job being better paid than his one at Fashion Street. With 120 members according to the *Jewish Year Book* for 1896/7, Great Alie Street had more than double the membership of Fashion Street. It also had a new architect-designed building.

The Federation, from its foundation in 1887, campaigned to encourage the amalgamation of smaller congregations and the re-building or renovation of religious premises. These buildings were often decrepit and sometimes downright unsanitary. Great Alie Street Synagogue was the seventh medium-sized model synagogue in the Federation's building

---

149   *JW*, 17th December 1897, p.201.

150   *JC*, 8th April 1898, p.12.

151   The *Jewish Chronicle* reported that David Applebaum read the April 1898 Passover services at Princelet Street Synagogue, under the aegis of the Princelet Street *chazan* Reverend Fassenfeld (*JC*, 15th April 1898, p.32). The *Jewish World*, however, reported that David Applebaum was officiating at the Passover services at Great Alie Street Synagogue (*JW*, 15th April 1898, p.57)! Reverend Applebaum cannot have been in two different synagogues at the same time. It is possible, though, that he might have officiated at a morning service in one synagogue and at an evening service in another. Or, as in the Diaspora, synagogue services are held on the first two days of the eight-day Passover festival, at one synagogue on the first day and at the other synagogue on second.

152   *JC*, 23rd September 1898, p.23; *JC*, 30th September 1898, p.21.

programme. Two congregations were merged. The first was the Kalischer Synagogue, a congregation that had been in existence since 1863.[153] As its name suggests, it had originally been formed by a number of fellow-countrymen, in this case poor immigrants from the town of Kalisz (in Yiddish, "Kalisch") in west-central Poland. Its small synagogue in Tenter Buildings, St Mark Street, had comprised only two rooms and was considered "unsafe and truly unsuitable for the sacred purpose for which it was intended".[154] The second and smaller congregation was one that had previously existed at Windsor Street, Sandy's Row. Like the Kalischer Synagogue, the Windsor Street Synagogue had been one of the founder members of the Federation.

The new synagogue was opened on 26th May 1895 by Sir Samuel Montagu MP, president of the Federation, and Dr Herman Adler, the Chief Rabbi.[155] The new building had cost £1,600, towards which members had collected £600, including from a Grand Evening Concert at Shoreditch Town Hall,[156] leaving the balance to be raised by further donations. Montagu, responding to the gift of a golden key in a morocco leather case, congratulated the members on their efforts but deplored the heavy debt that now hung over them. While Jews were liberal donors to charities, he remarked, they always seemed reluctant to support synagogues. However, he believed that if an earnest appeal were made, members would be able to wipe out the debt. A notice had appeared in the *Jewish Chronicle* before the synagogue opening appealing for funds[157] and now a second appeal was made.[158] The notices, placed by the secretary of the Federation, printed the names of donors together with

---

153   *JC*, 14th December 1894, p.14.
154   *JC*, 7th June 1895, p.3.
155   *JC*, 31st May 1895, p.14.
156   *JW*, 22nd February 1895, p.1.
157   *JC*, 17th May 1895, p.2.
158   *JC*, 7th June 1895, p.3.

the amounts of their contributions, in the case of the earlier notice, right down to individual half-crown (12.5p) donations. The appeals reduced the amount of the debt, but it was not wiped out, as Montagu had hoped.

Great Alie Street Synagogue was much more prepared to report its activities to the Jewish press than Fashion Street had been. As a result, in the years following David Applebaum's appointment, there are many mentions in the newspaper of his having officiated at this or that service. These include: *Rosh Hashonah, Yom Kippur* and a dedication service in 1898; *Rosh Hashonah* and *Yom Kippur* in 1899; Passover, *Shavuos* (Festival of Weeks), *Rosh Hashonah* and *Yom Kippur* in 1900; a memorial service on the death of Queen Victoria, Passover, *Rosh Hashonah* and *Yom Kippur* in 1901; and a memorial service in 1902.[159] After that mentions of him cease. In August 1903, the Synagogue placed advertisements for a reader and *Baal Korah* at an undisclosed salary, in two consecutive week's editions each of the *Jewish Chronicle* and *Jewish World*.[160] All the advertisements stipulated that a reader and *Baal Korah* was "Wanted Immediately". The Synagogue was closed at the time for repairs and structural alterations. When it reopened in September 1903 with a re-consecration service, David Applebaum did not officiate as reader.[161] His connection with Great Alie Street had by then ceased.

Great Alie Street Synagogue was a very traditional *shul* by comparison with the more anglicised community which David Applebaum had served

---

159   *JC*, 23rd September 1898, p.23; *JC*, 30th September 1898, p.21; *JC*, 16th December 1898, p.19; *JC*, 8th September 1899, p. 23; *JC*, 22nd September 1899, p.24; *JC*, 20th April 1900, p.26; *JC*, 8th June 1900, p.23; *JC*, 28th September 1900, p.27; *JC*, 5th October, 1900, p.19; *JW*, 8th February 1901, p.326; *JC*, 12th April 1901, p.26; *JW*, 27th September 1901, p.5; *JC*, 17th Jan 1902, pp.26-7.

160   *JC*, 7th August 1903, p.2; *JC*, 14th August 1903, p.2; *JW*, 7th August 1903 p.403; *JW*, 14th August 1903, p.419.

161   *JC*, 18th September 1903, p.30.

in Newcastle. At Great Alie Street, sermons were sometimes delivered in both English and Yiddish, for example at the re-consecration service, to ensure all congregants were fully engaged. We also read that in May 1904 the synagogue hosted a Friday afternoon sermon lasting "over three hours" from Reverend C Z Maccoby, the celebrated preacher, on the lessons of the Ten Commandments.[162] A fiery and emotional speaker and official *maggid* for the Federation of Synagogues, Maccoby could easily fill an East End synagogue with crowds of men and women thronging to hear lengthy, old-style oratory of a kind that had no place in anglicised, middle class congregations.[163] Nevertheless, for all the conservatism of the Great Alie Street synagogue, its congregation possessed sufficient kinetic spiritual energy for the synagogue's independent existence to continue until 1969, surviving to be one of the last functioning synagogues of the old Jewish East End.[164]

---

162 *JC*, 27th May 1904, p.27.

163 Reverend Maccoby's presence was also capable of causing a riot. In September 1896, he was due to speak at Sandy's Row Synagogue in the East End. The waiting crowd was so impatient to hear him that it broke down the outer iron gate in the rush to get in. His instructions were to preach in English. There were calls of "Yiddish, Yiddish" and then an uproar. Those objecting to English were asked to leave and "a violent commotion then ensued, and as the disturbance could not be quelled, the police were called and the synagogue cleared "(*JW*, 25th September 1896, p.6).

164 The Great Alie Street Synagogue, or Alie Street Synagogue as it came to be called after the name of the street changed, merged with Fieldgate Street Synagogue in 1969. During the life of the synagogue, the character of the area in which it was located changed from residential to light industrial and its congregation fell away. Since 1969, the area has changed again and is now on the edge of London's financial district. The synagogue, which its congregants laboured so hard to raise funds to build, has been demolished and its site is now occupied by an office block with a strip club at the ground floor level.

17. Maurice Applebaum and Peggy Grey

A joyous event that occurred during David Applebaum's employment at Great Alie Street was the marriage at the synagogue of his eldest son, Maurice, to the eldest daughter of Reverend Morris Grey. The wedding took place on 6th June 1899. In their marriage certificate, Maurice's age is given as 24 and that of his bride, Rebecca, who was known as Peggy, as 21. It was not only a union of the eldest children of two close friends, but may also have been a marriage between relatives, cousins of some degree. It was a marriage that would last for 64 years.

In 1893 or 1894, Morris Grey seized the opportunity to move from Newcastle to take up a position as reader with a small congregation in Poplar in East London. His background as a *chazan* up to this date, whether in the North-East or before that in Poland, is not known. His career in Britain was the very antithesis of that of his close friend. While David Applebaum moved from *shul* to *shul,* being associated with at least five synagogues between in England between 1886 and 1907, Morris Grey stayed put with the Poplar congregation for 35 years or so, right up until his death in 1929.[165]

Morris Grey must have realized he was taking a risk when he took up his appointment with a barely-established congregation. In the early 1890s, Poplar was beyond the eastern edge of the Jewish East End, an area which London Jews referred to as "the Far East". In 1891, a number of Jewish residents approached the United Synagogue movement for financial assistance in setting up an independent synagogue. They were rebuffed. The executive committee of the United Synagogue council rejected the application as premature. The Jews in Poplar were too

---

165   JC, 10th May 1929, p.11. The close relationship between the two *chazanim* continued throughout David Applebaum's life. In July1905, David Applebaum jointly officiated with his friend at Reverend Grey's daughter Rose's wedding at Poplar Synagogue (*JC*, 7th July 1905, p.33; *JW*, 28th July 1905, p.411.)

few in number and in any event lived within walking distance of the East London Synagogue, which could meet their religious needs.[166] The Poplar applicants nonetheless pressed on. A year later, a place of worship they established was being referred to "the Poplar Temporary Synagogue" and the executive committee, somewhat grudgingly, agreed to afford the congregation limited recognition by permitting the Poplar congregation to participate in United Synagogue burial arrangements, but only for a temporary three-year period.[167] In July 1894, the president of the Poplar Synagogue wrote to the *Jewish Chronicle* proudly stating that the synagogue had been in existence for three years, occupied premises capable of seating 60 men and 30 women, and, although some limited help from Sir Samuel Montagu had been gratefully received, the establishment of the new synagogue community was chiefly down to result of the efforts and resources of its members.[168]

The small, struggling congregation which Morris Grey joined as reader cannot have supplied him with much of an income. Nevertheless, seems to have thrown himself into the job, body and soul, fully participating in the life of the community. The *Jewish Chronicle* in November 1894 records that on *Simchas Torah* (the Rejoicing of the Law), the happiest of all Jewish religious festivals, Reverend Grey not only conducted the service, but also, at a reception afterwards in the Hebrew classes school room, organised his three daughters to render, with his assistance, a selection of Hebrew and English songs.[169]

Maurice Applebaum was the only one of David Applebaum's eight sons not to be born in Britain. At the date of Maurice's marriage, he, his bride,

---

166   *JC*, 10th July 1891, p.9.
167   *JC*, 11th March 1892, p.15
168   *JC*, 20th July 1894, p.7.
169   *JC*, 2nd November 1894, p.20.

his father and mother and his bride's parents were all Russian nationals. He made two applications for naturalisation as British citizen, the files on which are publicly accessible.[170] As a result of the material available in these applications, more is known about him during the first ten years of the twentieth century than anyone else in the Applebaum family.

Maurice's profession is described in his marriage certificate as "draper". The years after his wedding were a restless period. He and Peggy moved house five times between 1899 and 1904, all addresses located in the East End. He also started to call himself "Appleby" in this period, the first of the Applebaums to do so. Initially, he only used the anglicised form of his name for business and legal purposes and in other areas of his life, most particularly within the friendly society movement, continued to be "Applebaum". By 1905, he is no longer a draper and he is described as a jeweller in his first naturalisation application. A piece of his 1906 letterhead survives in the official file. He is by then trading as "M. Appleby & Co, Dealers in Gold, Silver, Platinum, Dental Alloy, Precious Stones". In essence, though, it was a scrap gold business. Old jewellery, false teeth, anything with a gold content was bought for scrap value and the precious metal extracted and re-sold.

Maurice's first application lapsed, but a second application was made in 1911. By then he was living with his wife and three children at 39 King Edward Road in South Hackney, north of the East End and near Victoria Park. It was a good address and the 1911 census reveals that the family kept two live-in servants. Maurice was a rising man and, certainly, none of his siblings ever paralleled his trajectory. The file on this later application contains a Scotland Yard CID Special Branch report. Maurice had done so well, so quickly, that he had made enemies. Two informants, a Dr Midloursky and a Mr van Couverden, accused him

---

170   National Archives, HO 144/999/126173.

of giving a bad cheque, of preparing paperwork for a false insurance claim and of receiving stolen goods. It says much for Maurice that the police, after investigation, rejected these allegations and characterised the informants as being themselves suspicious. Midloursky, indeed, the police believed to be "a secret agent" of the Russian government.[171] Scotland Yard's conclusion was that the informants had previously held responsible positions in some Jewish friendly and benefit societies and that Maurice "was the means of van Couverden and Midloursky being removed, and the latter do not try to conceal their bitter hatred of… [him]".[172]

Maurice Appleby had by this time become immersed in the Jewish friendly society movement, so much so that his wife, Peggy, would later complain that he often neglected a good business for the sake of these activities.[173] Purchasing scrap gold meant business travel and this brought him into contact with Jewish communities all over the country. Wide-ranging communal and commercial activities could therefore be combined. His first effort in these communal matters, and in which he involved his father and his siblings, was one very close to home, The Sons of Dobrin.

---

171 A statement which was less sinister then than it may now seem. Russia was by this time considered a friendly power, having been associated with Britain and France in the Triple Entente since 1907.

172 Maurice Applebaum had worked closely with Van Couverden and Midloursky in the Hebrew Order of Druids. In 1908, Van Couverden and Midloursky were respectively Grand President and Grand Vice President of the Grand Lodge of the society and Maurice Applebaum was Treasurer (*JC*, 14th February 1908, p.24).

173 Conversation with Brian Appleby, 1st November 1987.

18. The Sons of Dobrin

In the twentieth century, Britain became a modern welfare state. Citizens became entitled to a national system of free health care and to a cradle-to-grave financial safety net to protect them against extremes of misfortune. These developments took the place of charity, local welfare arrangements and mutual assistance.

Friendly societies were an important means of mutual self-help in Britain before the advent of the welfare state. They were associations of individuals whose purpose was to provide members with cash sums in specified circumstances. They could also be used as mechanisms for saving or making loans. As institutions, they had upsides and downsides. All funds accumulated were for members; no fees were extracted to generate profits and thereby dividends for shareholders. They were often small operations, which meant that members who so desired might find it easy to participate in management. On the other hand, they lacked economies of scale and were sometimes managed incompetently. Friendly societies might also have a social aspect, serving as clubs for the like-minded to meet in convivial circumstances.

In Britain, friendly societies came to be regulated by the Friendly Society Act 1896. Societies that registered were required to comply with certain requirements as to governance, accounting and audit. In return, they received legal and tax privileges. The friendly society movement in Britain was probably at its most diverse in the Edwardian period. By 1910, there were an astonishing 26,877 societies or branches of societies in the country.[174]

As British Jewry expanded, so did the number of mutual associations that met its needs. For poorer Jews, these associations were the most

---

174 *Encyclopaedia Britannica*, William Benton, London, Chicago, Geneva, Sydney, Toronto, 1963, Vol.9, p.845.

important social institutions after synagogues. Their variety and ubiquity challenge any attempt at a brief summary.[175] Most came to be regulated by the Chief Registrar of Friendly Societies, but some were not and fall outside official records. Multiple membership was also a feature with members spreading their financial risk by joining more than one society. It is therefore difficult to calculate just how many Jews in total participated in mutual associations. Some societies, usually the more venerable, existed to support religious practice, such as by paying allowances during periods of mourning or providing for religious burial. These were often administered through a synagogue and were an important reason for its existence. Other societies were secular, such as those with a socialist or Zionist tinge. Some were simple dividing societies, which collected money, paid it out on certain occurrences and periodically redistributed surpluses. Others were more sophisticated and accumulated capital to improve benefits for members. Some societies, like the Cracow Jewish Friendly Society (membership 380 in 1905), were originally based on the coming together for self-help of fellow countrymen in a strange land and were named after their town or city of origin. Others were linked to particular trades, like the Cigarette-makers and Tobacco Cutters Benefit Society (membership 100 in 1905).[176]

For the Jewish East End working man, friendly societies were the way in which he protected himself and his family against financial calamity. He might make an investment of three shillings (15p) a week, placing a shilling each with three different societies, and in return receive the promise from each of £50 on his death, £10 on his wife's death, and other amounts in other circumstances. This example was cited in a 1905 *Jewish*

---

175   For a more extensive description of the Jewish friendly society movement during this period see Black, op. cit., pp. 194-200.
176   Black, ibid.,p.199.

Chronicle feature on friendly societies.[177] But while the friendly society movement provided a useful safety net for many, it was not available to all. Some families were simply too poor to avail themselves of much in the way of mutual self-help. For those in working poverty, for example, a Jewish boot-finisher with average earnings of 16s (£0.80p) a week in 1898,[178] every penny counted and a three shilling weekly outlay would be quite beyond his means. And as for the level of pay-outs promised, many at the time were seriously concerned that these payments were beyond the capacity of most societies to deliver on a consistent long-term basis. Societies competed for members and the promise of high pay-outs was an inducement to join. Badly administered or overgenerous societies could easily tip over into bankruptcy with younger members finding that they had subscribed for future benefits that they would now never receive. Well-informed contemporaries were concerned that the system was precarious and urged reforms, including the federating or merging of societies, the cutting back on paid offices within societies, a less generous approach to benefits and the pooling of facilities.[179]

Leaving aside economics and finance, the societies provided a vibrant setting for social activity. They would be dominated by a responsible committee whose main function would be to decide whether or not to make cash grants in any case and, if so, how much. Inevitably, members would vie for office. Some societies resembled gentile lodges, with elaborate rituals, regalia, and grandiose titles. Others deliberately abjured such fripperies. But whether or not members engaged in the pleasures of dressing up and play acting, the typical Jewish friendly society was,

177   A. Rosebury, "The Jewish Friendly Societies: a critical survey", *JC*, 8th September 1905, pp.19-20.
178   *JW*, 7th January 1898, p.274.
179   Examples: *JW*, 11th November 1898, p.111; *JC*, 23rd October 1903, p.6; *JW* 10th February 1905, p.385; *JW*, 14th December 1906, p.666. Rosebury, ibid., p.20, listed a total of ten matters of concern on which the Jewish community should focus.

in the words of a knowledgeable observer, "continually throbbing with sociability, friendship, solace, and all the human emotions without which civilised life would be impossible".[180] He might have added, but did not do so, that they were also often hotbeds of argument, faction, personal rivalry and, when it could be afforded, litigation.

The Sons of Dobrin Benefit and Tontine Society was founded in about 1890. The word "tontine" in the society's name suggests its rules provided, after payment of benefits, that not all unused funds collected would be repaid as dividends and a small surplus would be retained for payment to its last surviving member. This provision would have been intended as a loyalty incentive.

The founder of the society was a Mr M Lazarus, an act for which the Society later honoured him with a medal.[181] The first mention of the Sons of Dobrin in the Jewish press was in November 1893, when it placed a notice in the *Jewish Chronicle* for someone to act as its secretary.[182] Lazarus was at the time its president and the society was based at his home. He is a puzzling individual. He was "Morris" Lazarus in the 1891 census and "Marks" Lazarus in his 1897 naturalisation application and later censuses. His occupation, as cited in official records, changed over a 20-year period from "tailor" to "clothier" to "estate agent auctioneer" to "jewellery dealer". Inconsistencies in information he provided to the authorities regarding the ages of members of his family make it difficult to establish when he first came to Britain. It was certainly no later than 1881 and may have been as early as 1878, which in the latter case would mean that he arrived in London at about the same time as David and Jeanette Applebaum. Clearly, there was some process afoot attracting

180   Rosebury, ibid., p.19.
181   *JC*, 6th March 1903, p.28.
182   *JC*, 17th November 1893, p.11.

Dobriners to London in the years *before* the pogroms and the May Laws and enough of them in the city within a few years to make the formation of a *landsmanshaft* feasible.

In the 1890s, the society included among its presidents a Mr S. Simmons and a Mr M. Clapper,[183] but in this period it seems to have fallen into the doldrums. Its revival was later attributed to the perseverance of its secretary, Mr J. Levy, in recognition of which, in December 1898, its members presented him with a testimonial.[184] It was at this time of the society's revival that Maurice Applebaum became involved with its activities and he soon came to dominate it.

Maurice Applebaum was a significant figure in the Jewish friendly society movement in Britain throughout his long life.[185] His first assay into the field was his involvement in the Sons of Dobrin. He arrived in London from Newcastle towards the end of 1895 aged about twenty. Within three years, he had become vice president of the society[186] and a year later its president.[187] The Sons of Dobrin came to have a strong family aspect, bringing together in-laws and other relations for joint activities. His aunt's husband, Nathan Bomberg, and his brothers, Isidore and Hyman, were actively involved. So too, but less deeply, was his father, Reverend Applebaum. Maurice's father-in-law, Reverend Grey, was a trustee of the society. Other officers were close friends of the family. Maurice was re-elected president of the society on a number of occasions and probably without interruption for the rest of the society's life.

---

183 *JC*, 6th March 1903, p.28.
184 *JW*, 30th December 1898, p.223.
185 *JC*, 1st February 1963, p.24.
186 *JW*, 30th December 1898, p.223.
187 *JC*, 22nd December 1899, p.27.

From the start, the Sons of Dobrin provided insufficient scope for Maurice's ambition. He soon began to take an interest in the wider Jewish friendly society world. In January 1900, he attended a friendly society conference on behalf of the Sons of Dobrin and became a member of a committee of delegates charged with drawing up a scheme for re-arranging the duties of friendly society medical officers.[188] The Sons of Dobrin comprised a single lodge, which, by 1903, had 132 members. Many of these would be members of several friendly societies and only a minority would have been born in Dobrin. However, by this time, Maurice's energies had become focused on a much larger friendly society, the Hebrew Order of Druids.

Outlandish names for friendly societies were common in late Victorian Britain. They were a reflection of the wish of members not to take themselves too seriously and have a little fun while pursuing worthwhile social objectives. Such names also reflected a desire to indicate that a society was not affiliated to any particular political party. Nevertheless, "Hebrew Order of Druids" was later felt to be an unsuitable name for a society aiming for a Jewish membership and the society was re-named "Order of Shield of David".[189] Founded in 1896, by 1903 it had grown to comprise ten lodges in London. By 1905, it possessed 18 lodges in Britain, plus one in Johannesburg, with a membership of 1,120 and a capital of £1,622.[190] It was to grow further in years to come.

Maurice seems to have thrown himself with a passion into being an organiser for the Hebrew Order of Druids. He brought to the task

188 *JC*, 19th January 1900, p.26; 2nd February 1900, p.26.
189 *JC*, 17th April 1914, p.28; JC, 9th October 1914, p.22.
190 *Grand Order of Israel and the Shield of David Friendly Society* Archives in the London and M25 Area, www.aim25.ac.uk/cgi-bin/vedf/ (accessed 20th May 2012); Rosebury, op. cit., p.19; Feldman, op. cit., p.318.

his connections with the North-East and the synergy of being able to combine business trips to provincial cities with organisational work. During 1903-5, he founded the society's Newcastle lodge and was involved in setting up lodges in Middlesborough and Leeds.[191] He was rewarded in 1905 by being elected Grand President of the Hebrew Order of Druids, an event which he celebrated by placing a notice in the *Jewish Chronicle* wishing the society's officers and members a happy and prosperous Jewish New Year.[192] In the same year, in its feature on Jewish friendly societies, *Jewish Chronicle* listed a number of "notable leaders" of the friendly society movement in Britain and named Maurice as one of them. He was only thirty and had come far.

The much smaller Sons of Dobrin remained in existence until its dissolution in 1912.[193] From Maurice Applebaum's arrival on the scene, a big feature of the Sons of Dobrin was its annual ball. The *Jewish Chronicle*'s report on the 1900 festivities[194] brings out quite clearly the extent to which the society's members and their families were devotees of the music hall. Some of the entertainers may have been semi-professional. Most would have been amateurs with some musical or comic talent, which they enjoyed the chance to exercise. These included Reverend Grey's three daughters, one of whom was Maurice's wife. Some of the amateurs would have had aspirations to tread the boards of variety theatres and looked to such occasions as opportunities to hone

---

191   *JC*, 3rd April 1903, p.32; *JC*, 26th February 1904, p.33; *JC*, 13th May 1904, p.32; *JC*, 24th February 1905, p.40.

192   *JC*, 29th September 1905, p.17.

193   The registration of the Sons of Dobrin Benefit and Tontine Society (registration no: 768) under the Friendly Societies Act 1896 was cancelled at its request on 2nd September 1912, pursuant to Section 77 of the Act (*London Gazette*, Issue no 28643, 10th September 1912, p.6740).

194   *JC*, 2nd March 1900, p.31.

their skills and create a following. David Applebaum's son, Isidore, who directed the entertainment, was already trying to make a career in show business.

"SONS OF DOBRIN BENEFIT SOCIETY:- A concert and ball to celebrate the anniversary of the establishment of the Society was given on Saturday evening at the King's Hall, Commercial Road, E under the direction of Mr I Applebaum. During the evening Mr B Peres, the Vice- President, on behalf of the Society, presented Mr M Applebaum, the President, with a gold medal and an illuminated address in recognition of the energetic work he had done for the Society. Mr S Isaacs, who also addressed the gathering, referred to the great progress that had been made during the year. The recipient responded in suitable terms. The following artists, to whom a hearty vote of thanks was passed, kindly gave their services: The Misses Lillie Vaine, Hannah Straus, Rose Grey, Jennie Venton, Sisters Grey, Little Gertz, Messrs Tom Star, Harry Leamore, H.Evans and the Alberto Troupe. Mr Harry Seymour recited "The Absent Minded Beggar", a collection being made for the War Fund. Sheere's Band was in attendance."

There is a supremely incongruous element to the evening. Maurice Applebaum and many others present were Polish-born, Yiddish-speaking, Russian citizens. Yet here they were at a *landsmanshaft* meeting listening respectfully to a recitation of a recently-composed fund-raising poem by Rudyard Kipling, then at the height of his popularity, and making a collection for the families of British soldiers who were away fighting the Boers. Most British Jews, and particularly the more anglicised among them, strongly supported British military action in the South African War. Support was a way of showing loyalty and patriotism and, for many, seems to have been genuinely felt. Many British gentiles with anti-war or pro-Boer sentiments subscribed to the view that the fight between the British empire and the Afrikaaner republics had only come about through the secret and self-serving machinations of Jewish financiers. It was a baseless view and is an early example of British left wing anti-Semitism.[195] It was also a view that conspicuous Jewish support for the British Empire war effort did nothing to dispel.

The Sons of Dobrin was to make another patriotic gesture in 1902, when it sent a loyal message of congratulation to King Edward VII on his coronation. Receipt of the congratulatory address is recorded among hundreds of others in the *London Gazette*.[196]

In the years that followed, the Sons of Dobrin continued its work of financial self-help, but its membership did not grow, probably declining somewhat in the years leading up to its dissolution.[197] The much larger Hebrew Order of Druids became the main vehicle for Maurice's activities within the Jewish friendly society movement. The Sons of Dobrin seems to have become more of a social club; the kind of society where members could meet periodically to engage in the fun of giving and receiving awards and dressing up.[198] Its jollifications could, nevertheless, still be used by Maurice to entertain his contacts in the wider friendly society movement. At the Sons of Dobrin's supper and ball in 1903, among

---

195 "This view, moreover, was not confined to a lunatic fringe but was common in respectable Liberal and Labour circles" (Endelman, op. cit., p.153). See also Feldman, op.cit., pp.265-6.

196 *JC*, 3rd October 1902, p.33; *London Gazette* (Special Supplement), Issue 27484, 20th October 1902, p.6638.

197 In 1910, the Sons of Dobrin was reported to have a membership "of over 100" (*JC*, 15th April 1910, p.34).

198 At the Society's annual banquet in 1901: "By special order all present wore black bows or ties, the Committee wearing purple and white rosettes" (*JC*, 1st March 1901, p.29).

those entertained by a bevy of amateur and semi-professional acts, were the grand president, grand secretary and grand treasurer of the Hebrew Order of Druids, the president of the Widows and Orphans Fund, the treasurer of the Menassah Ben Israel Society and a lodge president from the Order Achei Brith.[199]

David Applebaum did not stand aloof from his eldest son's activities, but one senses a lack of involvement deriving from a difference in temperament. He did not share Maurice's passion for communal politics, nor was he business-like in his affairs. With his easy-going ways, his love of music and its performance, David was more like his younger sons. He was nonetheless at his death a paid up member of both the Sons of Dobrin and the Hebrew Order of Druids. We know this from his grave. The stone states that he was a member of both societies [Illustration H], the reference to the Hebrew Order of Druids being a somewhat bizarre inscription on the gravestone of an orthodox Jewish clergyman.

---

199   *JC*, 6th March 1903, p.28.

In about 1898, David Applebaum and his family moved from No 75 to No 149 Whitechapel Road.[201] Both properties were on the north side of the street, No 149 standing at the corner of Whitechapel Road and St Mary Street. No 149 was to be David Applebaum's home for the rest of his life. The property the family occupied was demolished in the twenty-first century and a petrol filling station now stands on the spot. Across the road is the substantial structure of the East London Mosque, a testament to the way in which the ethnic composition of the neighbourhood has changed over a century; from immigrant Russian Jewish to immigrant Bangladeshi Muslim.

The 1901 census provides a further snapshot of the Applebaums' family life. The census, taken as at the night of 31st March/1st April 1901, reveals 13 people living in the family home, a number of rented rooms above a shop. There were three working adults: David and his sons Isidore and Hyman. Isidore's occupation is given as "actor" and Hyman's as "jewellery traveller". David Applebaum was always short of money, it is said. However, he was not so poor that he and Jeanette sent their three teenage daughters, Rose, Sarah and Annie, out to work, even though by then they had all left school. While it is possible that the girls did have jobs outside the house, but the family did not want to admit it, it is more likely that the girls stayed home and helped their mother with

---

200 Where no attribution is given in this section, the source of information is one of the respondents named in the Acknowledgements or the author's recollection of information provided by his father.

201 The family moved sometime between Leonard Applebaum's birth in 1897 and Maurice's wedding in 1899. In June 1900, auctioneers, A. Prevost and Son, put the freehold of No 149 up for sale. In their advertised sales particulars (*JC*, 8th June 1900, p.4), they stated that the rent received by the freeholder was £110 p.a. The tenant paying this rent is likely to have been the occupier of the ground floor shop, who in turn sub-let the upper part of the building to the Applebaum family. The amount of the sub-rent payable is not known.

the cooking and cleaning and waited to find husbands or have husbands found for them. The first to marry was Rose, in 1907.[202]

There may have been a little less overcrowding at No 149 in 1901 than there had been when the Applebaums lived at No 75 as there was now one less adult living at home. David's eldest son, Maurice, had left and had set up home with his new wife, Peggy, in Albert Square, about half-way between his parents' home in Whitechapel and his wife's parents in Poplar. At some stage he seems to have joined his father-in-law's synagogue, perhaps after his father left Great Alie Street in 1902, and in 1905 he was elected to the Poplar Synagogue's management committee.[203] After his departure, his younger brother, Isidore, was the eldest son living at home. By 1904, he too had left home and was living in Tredegar Square in Mile End. In November of that year he married Ida Bernstein, a shoe-maker's daughter. They would later work together as a duo in music hall.

The Applebaum family at 149 in 1901 lived hugger-mugger and on top of each other. Photographs of Whitechapel Road at the time reveal that, for most properties, there were three storeys of residential accommodation above ground floor shops. Assuming for the sake of an exercise in imaginative reconstruction that the Applebaums rented a total of six rooms, including a kitchen,[204] how might they have all squeezed in? David and Jeanette might have had one room, the two oldest sons a

---

202 Rose Applebaum married Harry Derfield, a commercial traveller. On registration of the marriage, she gave her age as 19, although she was about 24.
203 *JW*, 23rd June 1905, p.286.
204 In 1901, the census enumerator recorded that the Applebaum household fell within the "five rooms or more" category, but he may have been including their kitchen among the five rooms; there was no consistency in the way these matters were recorded at the time. It is quite possible therefore that the family had even less space than is suggested.

second, the four girls a third, the five younger boys a fourth, leaving the fifth room as a living room. Possibly some rooms were sub-divided by a curtain to make two separate sleeping spaces. Or possibly there was no separate living room at all, but just a room, used as a bedroom at night, where in the morning bedding was bundled up and moved to another room, leaving the room to be used during the day for other purposes. To a twenty-first-century British middle-class sensibility such living conditions seem horrendous. They certainly induced tensions in the home. There could be serious fights between brothers. It was a house full of noise: shouting, laughing, singing, arguments. There was not much affection of a physical kind: kissing, cuddling and embracing. With such a large brood, perhaps their parents were concerned about seeming to exhibit favouritism if they ever singled out any child for special consideration. Perhaps everyone in the house, as a matter of course, had their fill of physical proximity. Sometimes, Manny Appleby later related, his mother became so exasperated with the overcrowding and commotion around her she would thrust a hunk of sweet *chollah* bread at him and shout *gai!* (go!) and he would take the dry bread and run out to play marbles with other small boys in the street. In the East End, this is where most children played.

The circumstances of their upbringing left its inevitable mark on the Applebaum children. Like children in many very large families, they had to fight for their mother's attention and in consequence came to over-venerate her. It is noteworthy, however, that none of her twelve children who survived to adulthood had large families of their own; it was not an experience any of them wished to replicate. Most had no more than two children. The Applebaum brothers tended to be ruggedly individualistic and quarrelsome, but all their lives they prized and celebrated their close relationships with each other. A party trick at weddings and barmitzvahs in later years, after the early death of their brother Mark had reduced the number of brothers, was for them to a make a comic entry into the celebrations in a line on their knees as the Seven Dwarfs. The brothers in music hall also worked together, most notably in a travelling revue they put together after the First World War and, when "resting", as agents for their brother Maurice's business.

It was not a household where book-learning had much place. None of the Applebaum boys seem to have showed any interest in education. They probably could see little point in it. Scholastic drudgery was not a quick route to fame or fortune or getting girls. Instead, the Applebaum family home became a breeding ground of vaudevillian performance, indirectly nurtured by David Applebaum. He enjoyed secular music, particular opera. He would introduce fragments of arias into his cantorial performances. He probably went around his crowded and busy home, holding himself slightly above the fray, making ironic jokes and serenely humming to himself.[205] Somehow, somewhere in their overcrowded home he kept a piano. He certainly organised his younger sons to sing together, much the same as Reverend Grey did with his three daughters, and he would take them along with him to perform as a choir when he officiated at weddings. It was a classic Jewish showbiz background. Many American Jewish music makers or entertainers had cantors for fathers: Irving Berlin, Al Jolson, George Gershwin, Eddie Cantor. Although none of the Applebaum brothers was to achieve great or lasting success on the stage, seven out of eight brothers worked at least for a period in music hall, whether as singers, dancers, comedians, back-stage, front-of-house or a mixture of some or all of these.

---

205   The popular stereotype of a ghetto *chazan* was of a genial gentleman forever humming tunes, even in his sleep (*JW*, 4th November 1898, p.83). However, it would never have done for David Applebaum to have *whistled* a tune. The Applebaum family subscribed to a widespread Jewish superstition that whistling in a home would bring it bad luck. Many East European Jews believed that whistling attracted demons.

From the 1880s onwards, music hall in British towns and cities went through a transformation. Venues became more lavish and more respectable. As London expanded, so new music halls began to colonise the suburbs.[206] The entertainment offered became broader and more family-oriented; usually two shows a night at 6.30pm and 9.00pm. There was a decline in the number of individual comic acts and sentimental ballad singers and an increase in comic teams, sketch troupes, conjurors, jugglers and ventriloquists.[207] The existence of so many halls, large and small, dotted all over the city, some 64 by 1913,[208] made it a time of opportunity. As a biographer of Chaplin has written about this period: "All one needed was a modicum of talent for song, dance, some sort of physical dexterity or a novelty or some trained animals, or just some gumption and get up and go to find a job entertaining around town and further afield, up and down the land".[209] This bug bit all but one of the Applebaum brothers. The 1901 census indicates that the very first of those in the family to try to make a living on the stage was Isidore, to be joined in later years by Hyman, then Mark, and then four other brothers.[210]

206   Paul Bailey (ed.), *Music Hall: The Business of Pleasure*, Open University Press, Milton Keynes and Philadelphia, 1986, p.xi.

207   *Louis Rutherford, Managers in a Small Way: The Professionalism of Variety Artistes 1860-1914*, in Bailey (ed.), ibid., p.96.

208   Dave Russell, *Popular Music in England 1840-1914; A Social History*, 2nd ed., Manchester University Press, Manchester & New York, 1997, p.98.

209   Simon Louvish, *Chaplin: The Tramp's Odyssey*, Faber & Faber, London, 2009, p.7.

210   Isidore may have suffered some preliminary setbacks. Having been described in the 1901 census as an actor, in 1904, when he married Ida Bernstein, his occupation is given as "jewellery traveller". In 1906, Hyman Applebaum married Rose Arbiter, a publican's daughter, and gave his occupation as "musical artiste". In the 1911 census, Mark Applebaum gave his occupation as "variety artist".

The language used by the Applebaums at home at this time was Yiddish. Jeanette lived in England for a continuous period of over forty years but was never comfortable speaking in English. Outside the home, David Applebaum would mostly be using Yiddish in speaking to officials and congregants at Great Alie Street Synagogue or in going about his business as a *mohel* or *shochet*. His children would have spoken Yiddish and English outside the home and English only in the classroom at school. They may have been forbidden to speak Yiddish in the school playground. All of the children at home spoke English like natives. The older ones had by this time eliminated their Geordie accents, acquired during their years in Newcastle, which had been mocked by their Cockney schoolfellows when they first arrived in London in 1895.

To an extent, East End Jews lived in a self-contained world. They had their own communal language, they had their spiritual needs met by its many synagogues – there were at least 65 in London in 1903[211] – and their social life and financial support catered for by their many mutual benefit societies. But they were not cut off from wider British life. Their children became adept at switching between one culture and another and an anglicised elite relentlessly pressured East Enders to engage more fully with gentile society without losing their Jewish character. One way in which this occurred and which reflects the willingness of East End Jews to participate in British life was in relation to public events. That patriotic *landsmanshaft*, the Sons of Dobrin, was not atypical in its loyalty to the Crown. In March 1900, the East End experienced the same explosion of celebration as did the rest of London over the Relief of Mafeking. News reached London that the Boer siege of the town had been lifted by British columns and as the *Jewish World*[212] reported:

211 Gartner, op. cit., p.197.
212 *JW*, 25th March 1900, p.127.

*"As from the earth, flags and bunting sprung up everywhere....
Brick Lane, the Regent Street of Whitechapel, was thronged with a
mass of humanity... There was hardly a street wanting in flags, and
the "Lane" was full of them. Stalls, barrows, shops, costermongers,
fishmongers and clothes dealers, all were bedecked with red, white
and blue. It was a day of rejoicing."*

Manny Appleby's first memory, he later said, was of being a four-year
old carried on a brother's shoulders through cheering crowds of jubilant
Jewish East Enders. He was wearing a sailor suit and collected half-
pennies in his sailor hat.

The 1901 census occurred eight weeks after the death of Queen Victoria.
Although by Jewish law it is a sin to mourn on the Sabbath day, East
End synagogues were full on the first *shabbos* after her death with
congregants in sombre clothes and men in black ties. Black curtains
were hung around the Ark in synagogues and black material around
the Torah reading desk.[213] At Great Alie Street, Reverend Applebaum
intoned the service as usual, but the minister, Reverend Mendelsohn,
as paraphrased by the *Jewish World*,[214] gave a special address, expressing
gratitude for what Britain had done for the Jews:

*"The long reign of sixty-three years was the record of civic freedom
for the Jewish people. While the children of Israel was [sic] still
knocking at the door, and was [sic] still being refused free admittance
by many nations, here they could lay aside the wandering staff."*

David Applebaum's activities as a *chazan, shochet* and *mohel* produced
an unusual seven-day weekly work pattern. As a clergyman, he worked
on his congregants' day of rest. He would have sought to have a quiet day

213   *JW*, 1st February 1901, p.306.
214   *JW*, 8th February 1901, p.326.

before any day on which he was due to officiate at the synagogue, but this could be interrupted if there was a *bris* to be performed. His practice as *mohel* was the most remunerative of his activities, but it was not the one that shaped his week; this was his work as a *chazan*, which was regulated by the requirements of the Jewish religious calendar. Early autumn was the busiest time of the year for a *chazan* with *Rosh Hashonah*, *Yom Kippur* and *Succos* coming back-to-back. There was a potentiality for a conflict of roles, however, if a Jewish clergyman was both a *chazan* and a *mohel*. Synagogue officers might wish to have first call on a *chazan's* time, but his role as *mohel* took priority. By Jewish religious law, a circumcision must take place on the eighth day after the birth of a baby boy, even if that day falls on a Jewish festival. Circumcisions cannot be deferred or advanced to fit the convenience of others.[215] If a *chazan* was the only *mohel* in town then the circumcision would take precedence, but in a great metropolis, where there were many *mohelim*, a substitute *mohel* could be found, perhaps the *mohel's* assistant, if he had one, or perhaps another *mohel*, who would be happy to earn the fee and might return the favour sometime in the future.

At the date of the census, there were only a few days left to go before Passover and, when it came, David Applebaum would officiate to a full house, the *Jewish Chronicle* reporting that the Great Alie Street Synagogue was so overcrowded that additional accommodation had to be provided for male worshippers in the ladies' gallery.[216] Great Alie Street was a traditional synagogue: Yiddish-speaking by preference, socially conservative and religiously observant. How highly, one wonders, did congregants regard a *chazan* known to have a penchant for gambling?

---

215 A bris must be performed on the eighth day after birth, even if it is Yom Kippur, unless there is a health issue (conversation with Dr Morris Sifman, 20th June 2012).

216 *JC*, 12th April 1901, p.26.

The answer is that it probably did not matter very much as gambling, in its various forms, was so widely indulged in by Jewish East Enders as to be considered a normal and acceptable pastime, provided it was pursued in moderation.

East End Jews speculated on the Hamburg lottery, they bet on horses, and they were avid card-players, preferably for money to add spice to the game. New card games were constantly coming in or going out of fashion. Zangwill indicates in "The Children of the Ghetto" that the popular East End card games in 1892, his novel's year of publication, were "loo, 'klobbiyos', napoleon, vingt-et-un and especially brag. Solo-whist had not yet come in to drive everything else out".[217] Betting on horse races presented a problem, however, because off-course cash bookmaking was illegal. Bets had to be placed with illegal bookmakers, usually through "bookies' runners", go-betweens who would take a punter's stake to the bookie and bring back his winnings, if any. This is probably how Reverend Applebaum placed his notorious Yom Kippur bet. He also went to the race-track from time to time with his best friend, Reverend Grey. London's only race-track was at Alexandra Park and the two East End cantors would have gone to the track dressed in something else than the clerical garb they habitually wore.

In "Children of the Ghetto", Zangwill presents a second type of *chazan* in contradistinction to Greenbaum, the overworked and underpaid complainer. He is Rosenbaum, second reader at a West End *shul*. He is "a bit of a gambler and a spendthrift". He is kept on, however, because of his fine voice and for the sake of his family. Reverend Applebaum was far from being a disreputable figure and there is certainly no

---

217 Zangwill, op.cit., p.54. David Applebaum's favourite was the German game euchre (pronounced "ocker"), which resembles solo whist (conversation with Minnie Stein, 12th October 1988).

evidence that he gambled immoderately, but the point is made that most congregations did not appear to expect the same degree of moral example and scrupulous behaviour from their *chazan* as they would do from their minister or a visiting *maggid*. Provided *a chazan* avoided serious family scandal, desecration of the Sabbath and infringement of the dietary laws, much could be overlooked if he had a tuneful voice, was a quick and accurate reader of Hebrew and had a pleasant personality.

Great Alie Street Synagogue was less than half a mile from David Applebaum's front door. To get there, he would need to cross Whitechapel Road and Commercial Road, taking care to avoid dirtying his boots with filth from the streets. Traffic at street level in 1901 was still horse-drawn. Hay wagons pulled by dray horses came in stately procession down Whitechapel Road each day bringing feed from the country for London's tens of thousands of horses. Horses drew cabs, carts and all manner of conveyances. Electric tram services had yet to start in central London and a motor car was a rarity. If any of the Applebaums were to visit the Greys in Poplar, they would probably get there by a horse-drawn tram, which ran smoothly along rails recessed in the main roads. The quantity of ordure deposited by London's horses was immense. If left, it would be churned up with rainwater and soot from coal fires to produce sticky "London Mud". To limit this occurring, the authorities employed "street orderlies", usually teenage boys, to collect horse manure off the streets as soon as it was deposited.[218] Manny Appleby would often later tell how as a child he would watch, fascinated, as the street orderlies performed their dangerous work, fearlessly darting under horses heads and between the wheels of moving vehicles to scoop up manure in the noisy, bustling street. Overcrowding at home and the attractions of street life, constantly

---

218   W.J.Gordon, "The Cleansing of London", originally published in *Leisure Hour,* 1889, http://www.victorianlondon.org/health/disposal.htm (accessed 28th May 2012).

brought East Enders out of their houses on to the streets, their work, domestic duties and the weather permitting. Children from poor homes had nowhere else to play. The jobless and underemployed idled at street corners. David Applebaum would make his way through the East End's streets and labyrinthine alleys and passages to and from the synagogue or appointments. One sees him dressed in black, perhaps in a high hat and frock coat and, in any event, easily recognisable to all as a Jewish clergyman, weaving his way through the crowded streets to officiate at a service or *bris* or going off to the slaughterhouse. Sometimes, he would take one of his younger sons with him, to get the boy out of the house and to acquaint him with his father's work. (His son, Manny, was often spoken of as the son who might be a future *mohel*.) One readily imagines a small boy in a cap and knickerbockers scurrying along after him, carrying his father's bag.

David Applebaum ceased to be *chazan* of the Great Alie Street Synagogue towards the end of 1902. His departure may have been followed a period in which he did not have an appointment as reader of any synagogue and in which he relied solely on his earnings as a *mohel* and any occasional work as a *chazan* he could obtain.[219] The course of his career as a *chazan* in the remaining years of his life is unclear. Were it not for the content of death notices placed by his family in the Jewish press on his death in 1907, we would not know that David Applebaum ever came to be connected with St Mary Street Synagogue.

St. Mary Street, now renamed Davenant Street, is a short street connecting Whitechapel Road and Old Montague Street. The St. Mary Street congregation was in existence in 1892, at which time it is described as "new".[220] It applied to join the Federation of Synagogues and was admitted as a member in October 1894. At the time, the *shul* was located at 8 St Mary Street. According to a treasurer's and secretary's report, submitted to the board of the Federation, the synagogue was erected on the site of a disused workshop at a cost of nearly £200. It had 110 seats and 55 members, "whose members were steadily growing".[221] The congregation is described in the board minutes as the "Limciecz Synagogue", a spelling which is varied slightly to "Limcicz" in an 1895 loan agreement with the Federation.[222] Attempts to locate "Limciecz"/"Limcicz", have

---

219   In the annex to a letter dated 19th January 1903 written by the secretary of the Federation of Synagogues, Joseph Blank, to the Chief Rabbi and listing the names of independent *mohelim*, David Applebaum is referred to as "Mr" and not as "Reverend", whereas most other *mohelim* in the list were referred to as "Reverend", suggesting that David Applebaum was not at the time working as a *chazan* (LMA ACC 2893/074).

220   *JC*, 15th July 1892, p.12.

221   Federation board meeting, 28th October 1894, LMA ACC/2893/001.

222   Loan Agreement, 6th March 1895, LMA ACC/2893/323/001; Federation board meeting, 28th October 1894, LMA ACC/2893/ 001.

so far been unsuccessful. Matters are complicated by the reference on David Applebaum's gravestone, erected in 1907, to his having been reader of the "Lonshitz" synagogue. "Lonshitz" is easier to explain; it was the Jewish name for the small Polish town of Leczyca, which is about 80 miles west of Warsaw. There were natives of the town living in London during the period and they formed a *landsmanshaft*, the Lynchitzer Brotherhood Friendly Society, which merged with the Shield of Isaac Friendly Society in March 1904.[223] However, nothing has yet been found in the records of the Federation of Synagogues or the contemporary Jewish press linking the name of "Lonshitz", or any similar usage such as "Lenshitz" or "Lynshitz", to St. Mary Street Synagogue. One explanation is that "Lonshitz" on the tombstone is an error, a mishearing or inaccurate rendering of "Limciecz"/ "Limcicz". Another is that "Limciecz"/"Limcicz" is a misspelling of the name of the village of Lesmierz, three miles from Leczycz. It is possible that the founders of the *chevra* originated from this village but in a short time the congregation came to be called after the larger and better known nearby town.

St. Mary Street was not a large congregation. At its Passover service in April 1903, an enumerator counted the number of worshippers attending the synagogue, men, women and children, and the total was found to be 116.[224] It seems always to have been in financial difficulties. It borrowed modest sums from the Federation in 1895 (£30), 1900 (£50) and 1904 (£50),[225] but always seemed to drag its feet over repaying instalments. As early as September 1896, the secretary of the Federation wrote to the synagogue to say that St Mary Street "is the only Synagogue which

---

223   *JC*, 18th March 1904, p.30.
224   *JW*, 24th April 1903, p.87.
225   *JC*, 15th February 1895, p.9; *JC*, 18th May 1900, p.27; *JC*, 10th June 1904, pp. 24-5.

gives trouble with its repayments and this cannot be allowed".[226] Records of the secretary's correspondence for the following years, however, show that St. Mary's Road was not the only bad re-payer among Federation members, but it was probably the worst. Indeed, at about the time of David Applebaum's death in 1907, matters became so bad that the secretary instructed the Federation's solicitors to pursue the personal guarantors of the synagogue's 1904 loan, no repayments having been received by the Federation since March 1905.[227]

The size of the congregation made it a candidate for amalgamation, in the opinion of the board of the Federation. In December 1897, board members took it upon themselves in a Federation meeting, which was reported in the Jewish press, to have a discussion regarding the possibility of a merger between St Mary Street and the Dunk Street *shul*.[228] This provoked a well-written and testy letter to the *Jewish Chronicle* from the secretary of St Mary Street Synagogue. The board's discussion, he wrote, was the first any members of St Mary Street had heard of any proposal for a merger, which they did not support. Their congregation, he said, was perfectly happy to continue going it alone.[229] That the synagogue was left to go it alone, and still able to borrow from the Federation, is

---

226 J. Blank to S. Rosenberg, 21st September 1896, LMA ACC/2893/070.

227 J. Blank to Gilbert Samuel & Co, 18th February 1907 and 27th February, LMA ACC/2893/078. The intervention of the Federation's solicitors did the trick and an instalment of £5 was quickly paid. However, by October Joseph Blank was chasing the synagogue again over a further late repayment (J.Blank to S. Rosenberg 6th March 1907, 3rd October 1907, LMA ACC/2893/078).

228 *JW*, 17th December 1897, p.202.

229 *JC*, 31st December 1897, p.9. The president of the Dunk Street Synagogue wrote a similar letter to the *Jewish World* (*JW*, 24th December 1897, p.225). This may have been a coordinated response by officers of both the congregations to what they saw as high-handed behaviour by Federation board members.

a reflection of two things: the board's limited power to influence its independent-minded members and its desire to keep them in the fold.

In 1904, the St Mary Street congregation moved premises, from No 8 to No 3 St Mary Street. A lease was taken out for the new premises and a £50 loan obtained presumably to improve the building.[230] There is some evidence that St Mary Street Synagogue was closed for a while in 1903-4, perhaps relating to the change in premises. It is possible that David Applebaum's appointment as reader dates from the opening of the new *shul*. Its congregation may have felt it an appropriate moment to install a new *chazan*. It would not, however, have been the most lucrative of appointments. The impecunious congregation was less than half the size of David Applebaum's synagogue at Great Alie Street. The latter had 266 worshippers at its Passover 1903 service, by contrast to St Mary Street's 116.[231] His appointment at St. Mary Street would justify him styling himself as "Reverend", which was useful for his practice as a *mohel*, but his salary would have been a fraction, perhaps only half, of what he had previously been paid. In consequence, he and his family remained heavily dependent on his earnings as a *mohel*.

---

230   Consent to Lease, 12th August 1904, LMA ACC/2893/323/002; Loan Agreement, 18th October 1904, LMA ACC/2893/323/004.
231   The membership of the two synagogues during the period 1902/3 – 1907/8 (i.e. the Jewish years 5663 – 5668), as reported in the *Jewish Year Book* for each of those years, was as follows:
1902/3 – Great Alie Street - 105; St Mary Street – 60
1903/4 – Great Alie Street – 105; St Mary Street – 60
1904/5 – Great Alie Street – 105; St Mary Street – 60
1905/6 – Great Alie Street – 114; St Mary Street – 62
1906/7 – Great Alie Street – 114; St Mary Street – 62
1907/8 – Great Alie Street – 120; St Mary Street – 94

21. The Harris Prager Inquest

The death of a baby boy that David Applebaum circumcised in 1904 was to cast a shadow over the rest of his life. The circumstances are well-documented. The coroner's inquest into the death of the child was covered in a 300-word report in the *Jewish Chronicle*.[232] On the evening of Thursday, 7th April 1904 (and not 17th April, as misstated in the newspaper), David Applebaum performed a *bris* on a baby boy at his parents' home in Leopold Street in Mile End. The child's name was Harris Prager and his father, Barnett Prager, was a cap maker. It was usual for a *mohel* to make a preliminary call on a family to check that a child was well enough to undergo the operation. One assumes such a visit was made. Whether it was or not, Barnett Prager and his wife did not tell David Applebaum that there was haemophilia in the family. They may have known and did not say, but it is more likely that they were unaware of any genetic risk, if such existed. The possibility that they knew of any risk and told Reverend Applebaum about it is discounted. The best practice among *mohelim* was that if a family history revealed the presence of haemophilia then circumcision should not be performed.[233] David Applebaum was an experienced *mohel*, who is unlikely to have disregarded this sensible approach. In any event, the *bris* went ahead and resulted in a haemorrhage that David Applebaum was unable to stop. The baby "cried very much". A doctor was called and attended the child several times. He stopped the bleeding for a while, but it started again and on the Tuesday after the circumcision little Harris Prager, twelve days old, died from loss of blood.

---

232 *JC* 22nd April 1904, p.17. There was no press coverage of the inquest in the *Jewish World* or in two of the East End's local newspapers, the *East London Observer and Tower Hamlets and Borough of Hackney Chronicle* and the *Borough of Stepney and Poplar and East London Advertiser.*

233 Jacob Snowman, *The Surgery of Ritual Circumcision*, The Initiation Society, London 1904, p.48.

The description of the child's Kiev-born father, Barnett Prager, as a "cap maker", gives the impression that he was a humble piece worker or journeyman, which was not the case. He was a cap manufacturer working on his own account and probably by then already an employer of labour. He could certainly afford a nurse to assist his wife during her confinement. He was an up-and-coming man. The 1911 census records the four-person Prager family, plus a live-in servant, occupying a seven-room house in salubrious Clapton. A few years later, he became the master of a masonic lodge. This is not the profile of a man likely to be ignorant of the consequences of a haemophiliac child being circumcised had he been aware of the genetic risk of such a child being born.[234] One concludes, therefore, that he was unaware of any possibility of inherited risk. An alternative explanation is that there was no genetic element in the case. At least one in four cases of haemophilia are the result of new mutations.[235]

An inquest was convened at the Stepney Borough Coroner's Court two days after the death. Wynne E Baxter, the East London Coroner, presided. Lawyer, botanist and antiquarian, Baxter had a reputation for being a capable, no-nonsense official with a blunt questioning style. He was well-known for having conducted most of the inquests on victims of Jack the Ripper. Baxter had recent experience of presiding over inquests into deaths following Jewish circumcision and knew the right questions to ask. There is no mention in the report on the inquest that David Applebaum brought along a solicitor, which suggests that he felt

---

234 JC, 5th May 1916, p.21. The diagnosis of haemophilia, which was made in respect of baby Harris, did not deter the Pragers from having further children. These were both daughters, the younger of which died shortly after her birth in July 1910, a second domestic tragedy for the Prager family.

235 See the discussion of haemophilia in the British royal family in Jane Ridley, Bertie; A Life of Edward VII, Chatto & Windus, London, 2012, p.6.

he needed no legal representation, probably because he knew that the doctor who attended the child, and who was to be called as a witness, was not going to criticise the conduct of the circumcision. There is also no mention in the report that David Applebaum required the services of a translator, indicating that he felt sufficiently confident in his English to hold his own in front of the coroner.

The first witness at the inquest was Barnett Prager, who described the broad facts of his son's death and does not appear to have attributed blame to anyone. The next was the nurse, Jane Davis. An important piece of evidence she supplied in answer to a question from the coroner was that after the circumcision the dressings on the child had not been interfered with in any way. Jewish circumcisions usually heal quickly. However, anxious mothers sometimes ignored a *mohel*'s advice and disturbed a dressing to check on progress. This could lead to renewed bleeding or, where the family lived in overcrowded and unsanitary conditions, infection.

The third witness was David Applebaum. He told the coroner, according to the press report, that he was "a certificated Mohel". The statement was intended to give some assurance to the court, but he was not one of the *mohelim* authorised by the Initiation Society, whose names the society published periodically in the Jewish press. It is likely that he was referring to a certificate he received from the Chief Rabbi when he first took up his appointment as a *chazan* in Newcastle in 1886 and which authorised him to act a *mohel*[236]. He told the coroner that he had been

---

236 These certificates seem originally to have been easily given and in February 1886 the Initiation Society suggested to the Chief Rabbi, Dr Nathan Adler, that in future before he gave such certificates he first extract from *mohelim* a promise to abide by the rules of the society (*JC*, 12th February 1886, p.12). It is not known whether David Applebaum was ever asked to give such a promise.

practising for 22 years, which indicates that his training was completed when he was in Lautenburg, Germany, in the early 1880s. He said that he had performed over 9,000 operations without having any trouble before. This corresponds to an average of almost eight circumcisions a week every week throughout the period. This rate of operations is credible as regards the years he was living and working in the East End,[237] but not during 1886-94, when he was serving the small Jewish community in Newcastle. As for having had no previous trouble, this is difficult to believe on statistical grounds. In late 1940s Britain, when by contrast with the Edwardian age, there had been improvements in social welfare and medical science, it was estimated[238] that 2% of all children circumcised as hospital out-patients would subsequently be admitted on account of haemorrhage or other untoward event. We must assume, therefore, that if David Applebaum had indeed performed 9000 circumcisions by 1905, he had seen serious problems before and probably fatalities.

The clinching evidence at the inquest, as far as David Applebaum was concerned, was that given by Dr George Black. He told the inquest that death was due to syncope, that is faintness or exhaustion, from loss of blood consequent on circumcision. Baxter asked the doctor point blank: "Was there any want of skill on the part of the *mohel*?" Dr Black gave an unequivocal response: "I think the operation was perfectly well done. In my opinion the deceased was a haemophilic subject".

---

237 In a letter to the *Jewish Chronicle* (6th February 1903, p.10), the secretary of the London Association of Mohelim proudly stated that the seven *mohelim* that made up the society, and who included David Applebaum, had performed 3000 cases in the previous year, which averages out at over eight circumcisions per *mohel* per week. In the same year, a *mohel* told a coroner's inquest (*JW*, 9th January 1903, pp. 288-9) that he had performed 350 circumcisions in the previous six months, which is an average of about 13 per week.

238 Douglas Gairdner, "The Fate of the Foreskin: A Study of Circumcision", *British Medical Journal*, Volume 2, 24th December 1949, pp. 1433-1437

The Coroner wound up by remarking that the circumcision performed on the child was a religious rite, which had to be performed, and that the *mohel* was an experienced official and duly qualified. The jury returned a verdict of "death by misadventure". Baxter certified the cause of death to the registrar of Mile End Old Town registration district as follows: "Violent syncope from loss of blood due to circumcision skilfully performed on a haemophilic subject". David Applebaum was exonerated. Unfortunately for him, that was not the end of the matter.

22. The Jewish "Circumcision Scandal" in Edwardian Britain

It was David Applebaum's professional misfortune that the death of Harris Prager should have occurred during a period of serious concern among British Jews regarding the activities of *mohelim*. A perception developed that the number of deaths as a result of circumcision was increasing among poor, immigrant Jews. The cause of the increase was considered to be negligence by ignorant or careless *mohelim*. In 1903, the *Jewish Chronicle* captioned letters to the newspaper on the subject "the Circumcision Scandal".

In 1900, the Chief Rabbi, Dr Hermann Adler, started to be pressed publicly by members of the community to take steps to reform the health and safety aspects of religious circumcision. A Mr F. S. Cohen, whose grandson had died of blood poisoning after circumcision, went to see the Chief Rabbi to persuade him that circumcisions should only be conducted by suitably-qualified doctors. He did not get the positive response he hoped for and wrote to the *Jewish Chronicle* to bring the matter to the attention of the Jewish public.[239] His comments evoked a supportive letter from a Dr Bernstein, who said that he had gone to see the Chief Rabbi two years before on the same issue.[240] The secretary of the Initiation Society responded to Cohen's letter.[241] *Mohelim* who were authorised by the society and whose names were available to the Jewish public had for many years been subject to rules which required them to carry out circumcisions "on strictly antiseptic principles", he wrote. As for only allowing doctors to carry out such operations, "however desirable such an arrangement would be, practical difficulties stood in the way of carrying it into effect." These included the lack of surgically-qualified *mohelim* in some provincial communities. Cohen came back with an attack on the Initiation Society, accusing it of being useless

---

239   *JC*, 22nd June 1900, p.8.
240   *JC*, 29th June 1900, p.8.
241   Ibid.

and powerless and incapable of acting as an effective regulator.[242] His views on circumcision were echoed by others, including "Provincial", an anonymous correspondent, who wrote[243]:

"I agree with Mr F.S.Cohen... "Unfortunately I lost my little son from this cause [i.e. blood poisoning]. It seems that in the Provinces, the operation is performed mostly by Chazonim, who understand very little if anything of antiseptic surgery. I know, that although a basin, towel and water were prepared for the Mohel who came to operate on my little son, they were never used, and that he came into my house after operating on another child, and left it again without washing his hands".

The competence of *mohelim* might have remained a low level communal concern for a little longer except for a report on the front page of the *Evening Standard* on 1st February 1902 on an inquest that had taken place earlier that day on the death of Lipman Fisher, the ten-day old son of a Bethnal Green boot finisher. The inquest was held at the London Hospital and the coroner was Wynne E Baxter. The report gives the impression that this was the first case of its kind to be investigated by Baxter. It had probably just been a matter of time before such a case would have come before him. The mounting population of Jewish poor in London was producing more births of poor Jewish children, more circumcisions and hence more deaths after circumcision, whether caused by haemorrhage or post-operative infection.[244]

---

242   *JC*, 6th July 1900, p.8.

243   *JC*, 6th July 1900, p.9.

244   London was not alone in having these problems. In New York, the rising number of deaths after circumcision among recent Jewish immigrants had been identified as a problem as early as the mid-1890s (*The Lancet*, 9th February 1895, p.363.)

The facts of the Lipman Fisher case were that after the baby's *bris*, the *mohel*, Simon Goldstein, had been unable to stop the child bleeding, even though he tried for three hours to do so. He was reluctant to call a doctor. Finally, the baby's father slipped out without telling Goldstein where he was going and went to the London Hospital to get help. The baby was then taken into hospital, where he died the next day. There appears to have been some discussion at the inquest as to whether what was described as "the Jewish manner" of circumcision was consistent with secular medical practice. Baxter was, however, keen to stay out of this territory. He remarked that when a religious element entered into a case, it was necessary to deal with it as carefully as possible. He nevertheless rebuked the *mohel* for not having called a doctor when the baby started to haemorrhage. The jury returned a verdict of "death by misadventure".

The report of the case stimulated more letters to the *Jewish Chronicle* from proponents for reform, including a strong one from F. S. Cohen in which he alleged that the Jewish establishment was trying to perpetrate a cover-up of a communal scandal.[245] The president of the Initiation Society, Louis Montagu, then entered the fray to describe the work undertaken by his society. This included the appointment of a doctor with the special object of instructing and examining *mohelim* to ensure that circumcisions were conducted "in accordance with the requirements of Surgical Science", the publication of a list of *mohelim* belonging to the society and a strict requirement that its *mohelim* involve a doctor promptly if haemorrhaging occurred.[246] The indefatigable Cohen responded[247] to question how it was thought possible to teach laymen to do operations that ought to be conducted by surgeons. The Initiation

---

245   *JC*, 7th February 1902, p. 8.
246   *JC*, 14th February 1902, p.6.
247   *JC*, 21st February 1902, p.7.

Society, he wrote, "is absolutely worse than useless, as it publishes a list of so-called operators, many of whom were absolutely incapable, and who would not be employed if they did not belong to the Society..."

The Society for Relieving the Poor on the Initiation of their Children into the Holy Covenant of Abraham, or Initiation Society, as it was generally known, dates back to 1745. It continues to exist and is the oldest Jewish charity in Britain. At the turn of the twentieth century, it was one of the communal organisations, like the Federation of Synagogues, dominated by the Montagu family. Louis Montagu, its president, was Sir Samuel Montagu's eldest son and was an unbending man of strong opinions. His father was raised to the peerage as Lord Swaythling in 1907 and, on his death in 1911, Louis Montagu succeeded not only to the title but also to the presidency of the Federation of Synagogues. He was less religious than his father, was unable to understand Yiddish and had less affinity than his father with Jewish East Enders. But like his father, he was prepared to fund communal organisations out of his own pocket. The annual reports of the Initiation Society over a number of years show that the society was only able to balance its books through financial support from its president, who also served as its treasurer.[248]

The overall objective of the Initiation Society was to ensure that Jewish boy babies were circumcised in accordance with Jewish law so that their fathers might fulfil their religious obligations in this respect and their sons could in due course take up their roles as adult males within the Jewish community. To this end, and as summarised by Louis Montagu in a public appeal for funds in April 1902,[249] the society carried out

---

248 There were deficits in the annual accounts of the Society throughout the period, as reported at annual meetings of its members in 1903 (*JC*, 23rd March 1903, p.22), 1904 (*JC*, 11th March 1904, p.30), 1905 (*JC*, 5th May 1905, p.32), 1906 (*JC*, 23rd February 1906, p.22) and 1907 (*JC*, 1st March 1907, p.25).

249 *JC*, 18th April 1902, p.9.

two types of work. One was the instruction of *mohelim*. The other was charity work among the poor. This charity work included the provision of free circumcisions, often for Jewish children born in workhouses. Cash grants were also made to parents on circumcision, it being recognised that some parents were so poor that they could not provide the essentials to keep a newly circumcised baby healthy and alive. In later years, nursing help would also be arranged. This charity work was valuable but relatively modest in scale. The 1902 Annual Report recorded a total of £232 being paid in grants. In the previous year the total had been £200.[250] As for free circumcisions, these seem to have been fairly few. During 1901, some 221 cases were "relieved" during the year,[251] but not all included the provision of free circumcision. By comparison, thousands of non-charity circumcisions were taking place each year within the Jewish population, many of these for poor parents who were unable to obtain any charitable assistance.

The society also made available to the public and published from time to time a list of *mohelim* who were members of the society. The list, as published in February 1901,[252] comprised 27 mohelim, 19 in London, five in the provinces and three in the colonies (Jamaica, New Zealand and South Africa). The *mohelim* were of two sorts: those who had been trained and examined by the society's medical instructor and those who had been otherwise trained, but who had been examined by the medical instructor and approved as to their proficiency. Among those *mohelim* who did not belong was to the society was David Applebaum. There were several good reasons why some *mohelim* might choose not to get involved with the Initiation Society. Many who had trained and qualified on the Continent saw no reason to submit to registration with the society or undertake to comply with the Society's rules. In particular,

250   *JC*, 11th April 1902, p.29.
251   *JC*, 23rd May 1902, p.14.
252   *JC*, 15th February 1901, p.2.

the Initiation Society did not permit advertising, which was an essential element in the practice of many commercially-oriented *mohelim*. The society also forbade its members from circumcising gentiles, a small but lucrative and growing market. As for the sons of parents where the father was Jewish and the mother was not, these are classified as non-Jews under Jewish law and could not be circumcised by Initiation Society *mohelim*.[253]

The records of the Initiation Society for this period were destroyed in a German air raid in the Second World War. It is, however, possible to track the change in emphasis in its activities from material appearing in the Jewish press, particularly summaries of its annual reports and meetings of members. From the beginning of the century, the society sought to upgrade its role in the medical training and supervision of *mohelim*. In 1901, it amended its rules to provide for the appointment of a medical officer to train *mohelim*, but was at first unable to find a candidate with the necessary qualifications who was prepared to undertake the work for the salary promised.[254] It was forced to rely on

---

253 Reverend Tertis, one of the most commercially successful *mohelim*, advertised "Surgical Cases attended to in Gentile families" (*JC*, 1st May 1903, p. 36). Circumcision among gentiles for health reasons was becoming more common in Britain during this period, the operation being strongly advocated by several eminent surgeons (e.g. E. Harding Freeland, "Circumcision as a Preventive of Syphilis and Other Disorders", The Lancet, 29th December 1900, pp.1869-1871; J. Bland-Sutton, "A Lecture on Circumcision as a Rite and as a Surgical Operation", *The Lancet*, 15th June 1907, pp.1408-1412.). The rule forbidding Initiation Society *mohelim* from circumcising gentiles was longstanding (*JC*, 12th February 1886, p.12). However it could be relaxed with rabbinical consent where the mother was undergoing conversion (*JC*, 21st April 1899, p. 21).

254 *JW*, 18th April 1902, p.65; *JC*, 11th April 1902, p.29. The Society wanted an instructor who was a qualified doctor, an experienced *mohel* and religiously observant. Such a paragon could not be found for the £100 p.a. offered and the society was compelled to offer a higher salary to candidates.

134

a temporary appointee, who provided lectures on antiseptic surgery to *mohelim*. At the request of the Chief Rabbi, Dr Hermann Adler, these lectures were extended to non-member *mohelim*.[255]

Once roused to action, Adler became a leading force in addressing concerns about the inadequacies of *mohelim* and transforming the Initiation Society into something akin to a regulatory body. He had been particularly exercised about the Lipman Fisher inquest and shortly afterwards suspended the *mohel*, Simon Goldstein, until he had been examined as to his competency by the Initiation Society's medical instructor. Adler and the *Beth Din* had no statutory authority to suspend Goldstein; their authority was religious and communal, but it was sufficiently compelling for Goldstein to acquiesce to his suspension. Adler also wrote to the secretary of the Federation of Synagogues on 13th February 1902 asking that members of the Federation furnish him with the names and addresses of all *mohelim* practising "in the East End and other districts". These *mohelim* would then, he said, be examined by the Initiation Society and the names of those who passed the society's examination would be published.[256]

The Chief Rabbi's request for the Federation's assistance came at a time of *rapprochement* between Adler and the United Synagogue, on the one side, and Sir Samuel Montagu and the Federation of Synagogues, on the other. The Jewish community felt itself under siege from mounting agitation for curbs on Jewish immigration and a general increase in popular anti-Semitism. Against this background, Reverend Avigdor Chaikin, a Federation rabbi, was invited to attend the Chief Rabbi's *Beth Din* and the Federation was allowed representation on certain communal

---

255 *JC*, 11th April 1902, p.29.
256 The text of the Adler's handwritten letter, as subsequently published, is set out in Appendix D.

bodies.[257] Adler's request for help on the *mohelim* issue seems to have become entangled with the politics of communal re-alignment. His letter was received in time for the Federation's March 1902 board meeting, but was not tabled for discussion. Dealing with the letter was deferred until Adler had reverted to the Federation with certain assurances it had sought over Chaikin's appointment to the Beth Din. The board wanted to know that Adler's attempt to reach out to the Federation was backed by the honorary officers of the rival United Synagogue, some of whom were opposed to anything more than a limited involvement by Chaikin in the Chief Rabbi's ecclesiastical court.[258]

The assurances requested were in due course received and at a board meeting on 14th July 1902, the Chief Rabbi's letter was finally considered, five months after its initial receipt. It was the only occasion during 1902-5 that the board of the Federation is recorded to have discussed the issue of Jewish ritual circumcision. As requested by the Chief Rabbi, the board resolved to circulate the letter to member synagogues.[259] The text of the letter was also published in full in the *Jewish World*.[260] Unfortunately, part of the letter was by now out of date. In it, Adler had stated that he had suspended the *mohel*, Simon Goldstein. However, in the five months during which the letter had sat in a Federation in-tray, Goldstein had been examined by the Initiation Society, found to be satisfactory, and been permitted return to practice. Goldstein promptly wrote to the *Jewish World* to point out this discrepancy.[261]

257   Black, op. cit., p. 289.
258   Correspondence between the honorary officers and the Chief Rabbi, LMA ACC/2805/03/01/005.
259   Federation board meeting, 14th July 1902, LMA ACC/2893/001.
260   *JW*, 18th July 1902, p.330.
261   *JW*, 25th July 1902, p.346.

Adler wished to get the Initiation Society to take on a more significant communal role. A limiting factor was its lack of financial resources. The society only managed to get by through the philanthropy of its president and treasurer and from donations and bequests from the rich.[262] An appeal to the Jewish public for support had disappointing results.[263] Finance, or rather the lack of it, was at the core of the "Circumcision Scandal". Few Jews would have objected if all Jewish circumcisions in Britain were conducted by Jewish, religiously-observant, medically-qualified *mohelim* – but who was going to pay for such a thing? As the *The Lancet* in 1905 in an article on circumcision among poor Jews put it: "There are many and great obstacles to providing medical men for all cases of circumcision, all of which are summed up in the simple statement that many of the patients' parents could never pay the medical operators a professional fee even on the lowest scale".[264] Poor Jews could only afford the services of non-medically-qualified *mohelim* and the Jewish middle class was unwilling to pay for or subsidise the medical

262 The society received some financial support from Lord Rothschild (*JC*, 5th May 1905, p.32). However, its finances were not to any extent restored until it received a £200 legacy from the estate of the deceased financier, relative and business associate of the Montagus, Ellis A Franklin, in 1909 (*JC*, 14th May 1909, pp. 7-8; *JC*, 17th December 1909, p.10; *JC*, 8th April 1910, p.33). For Franklin's connection with the Montagus see Chaim Bermant, *The Cousinhood; the Anglo-Jewish Gentry*, Eyre & Spottiswoode, London, 1971, pp. 281-3.

263 The public appeal for funds by the president of the Initiation Society in 1902 raised "a little over £100" (*JC*, 27th March 1903, p.22). Black, (op. cit. p.189) commenting on the Initiation Society's healthy balance sheet in the mid-1890s, states that this "reflected Anglo-Jewish generosity where important Jewish ritual was concerned". By the early 1900s, however, communal generosity does not seem to have kept pace with the expenses of the Initiation Society. Additionally, it is possible that the bad publicity which the society was getting in the correspondence columns of the Jewish press inhibited charitable support.

264 "The Danger of Circumcision Among Poor Jews", *The Lancet*, 16th December 1905, pp. 1796-7.

circumcision of the sons of their poorer co-religionists. They would not even adequately fund the Initiation Society in its modest charitable work. There was little practical alternative but to develop a corps of *mohelim*, unqualified medically but trained by doctors, who could provide an affordable service to the poorer members of the community. The Initiation Society would be the means for training and regulating these *mohelim* and it would just have to find the money to do so as best it could as it went along.

A year after the Lipman Fisher case, in January 1903, an inquest was convened by the Westminster Coroner's Court into the death of Michael Dosternok (or Pasdenock; there was uncertainty about pronunciation), the son of a Polish-born tailor living in Soho.[265] The child had been circumcised by Simon Goldstein, the same *mohel* who had circumcised Lipman Fisher, and who had now resumed his practice. After the *bris*, baby Michael bled profusely. Goldstein treated the wound with a powder chiefly composed of Fullers Earth, an industrial absorbent. A doctor, who was called, found the child to be in an extremely dirty condition with unclean and improperly fastened dressings, the evidence pointing to neglect by the parents. Five days after circumcision, the child died. A post-mortem examination was held and the child was found to be "undersized and in a very poor state of health". The cause of death was attributed to septic poisoning and improper treatment of the wound. The coroner was John Troutbeck, who was to garner a reputation as a self-confident official, unafraid to take on vested interests, particularly in the medical profession.[266] He was determined to get to the bottom

---

265 The *Jewish World* sent a reporter and, trumpeting its story as an exclusive, covered the hearing in great detail (*JW* 2nd January 1903, p.272 and 9th January 1903, pp. 288-9). It was not covered at all by the *Jewish Chronicle*

266 David Zuck, "Mr Troutbeck as the Surgeon's Friend: The Coroner and the Doctors – An Edwardian Comedy", *Medical History*, 1995, 39, pp.259-287.

of the matter. Troutbeck seems to have had no previous experience of infant death following Jewish circumcision. He wanted to know how *mohelim* were appointed, what their qualifications were supposed to be and who supervised them. The inquest was adjourned for further evidence and Goldstein was bound over in the sum of £20 to appear at the adjourned inquest. The practice of *bris millah* among British Jews was now on trial.

The resumed hearing was attended by a number of Jewish notables. *Dayan* Hyamson, deputising for the Chief Rabbi, explained how *mohelim* were appointed and trained by the Initiation Society and the rules to which they were subject, including those relating to personal cleanliness, and the need, in serious cases, to involve a doctor. The Initiation Society's temporary medical instructor, Dr Blok, told the inquest that in the East End there were two types of mohelim. The first type belonged to the Initiation Society. About eight or nine of these were medically qualified and the rest, about twenty, were unqualified. The second type comprised "several" *mohelim* in the East End, who neither belonged to or had been examined by the Initiation Society. Blok told the coroner that Goldstein had previously been suspended but after an examination had been deemed competent to carry out his duties; however, said Blok, Goldstein had now been suspended again by the Chief Rabbi.[267] In their respective evidence, Blok and Goldstein disagreed as to whether Goldstein had ever been told he should not use Fullers Earth to staunch bleeding.

The hearing seems at times to have been shambolic, mainly because no one had thought beforehand to provide a translator for the deceased

---

267   A notice from the Initiation Society was published shortly after the inquest stating that, acting upon instructions of the Beth Din, the certificate granted to Simon Goldstein had been withdrawn (*JW*, 6th February 1903, p.371).

child's parents. In the end, *Dayan* Hyamson had to act as translator. The inquest did not cover the Jewish community or its institutions with glory. Goldstein gave the impression of being a dangerous ignoramus. The coroner was dismissive of his alleged expertise. "In this case", he said, "there is ample testimony of looseness in working arrangements and even now Mr Goldstein does not seem to realise the importance of the antiseptic methods in modern surgery". He then criticised the Jewish authorities. Mr Goldstein had been in trouble before "and there should have been great precautions before licensing him to operate again." The jury, without leaving the box, returned a verdict of "death by septic poisoning, but how caused there is not sufficient evidence to show".

In the months that followed the circulation of the Chief Rabbi's letter to Federation member synagogues in which he asked the East End *chevrot* to name names, he received little information back. Perhaps the East End was less concerned about negligent *mohelim* than Dr Adler. Or perhaps there was a reluctance to behave like a *moiser*, an informer, against the *mohelim* who lived and worked in the midst of the Jewish East End, many of whom were also the respected *chazanim* of local synagogues. The Dosternok/Pasdenock case galvanized the Chief Rabbi into further action and within days of the inquest being reported in the *Jewish World*, he wrote again to the Federation. Its secretary, Joseph Blank, replied by return, expressing regret for the inadequate response of members, and saying that he had already "taken measures" to get Dr Adler the names he was seeking.[268] *Within three days*, Blank reverted to the Chief Rabbi with a list of twelve names, together with the addresses of the *mohelim* concerned.[269] At the top of the list was David Applebaum's name.

There is no doubt that the Dosternock/ Pasdenock inquest was a profound embarrassment to the Chief Rabbi and the Initiation Society. It prompted further critical correspondence in the Jewish press.[270] An editorial in the *Jewish World* observed, despairingly, that its report on the inquest made disagreeable reading and there seemed to be no plan that could be suggested to avoid a repetition of this kind of case.[271] At the same time, the secular authorities began to take a far greater interest in deaths after Jewish circumcision. Within six weeks of reports of the Dosternock/Passdenock case appearing, two inquests were held into the deaths of Jewish newly-born in which the role of Jewish circumcision

---

268   J.Blank to H.Adler, 13th January 1903, LMA ACC/2893/074.
269   J.Blank to H.Adler, 16th January 1903, LMA ACC/2893/074. The list of *mohelim* provided by Blank is in Appendix F.
270   JC, 16th January 1903, p.9; JW, 23rd January 1903, p. 321.
271   JW, 16th January 1903, p.298.

was an issue. In the first, the case of Marx Gripper, it was concluded that the child had died of blood poisoning. The poverty-stricken Gripper family lived in a filthy East End cellar and had used a dirty shawl as a bandage. The coroner stated that there were not the slightest grounds for criticising the *mohel* for the manner of the operation.[272] The second case, that of a child surnamed Finer, was also found to be the result of blood poisoning. The jury seemed keen to discover whether there was any link with the circumcision, but the coroner was emphatic that he saw no connection.[273] Again, the *mohel* was exonerated.

With Jewish circumcision under greater scrutiny, some further form of regulation seemed likely. Some *mohelim* outside the Initiation Society, and who wanted to remain that way, organised themselves into a "London Association of Mohelim". It comprised seven *mohelim* and included David Applebaum. Its secretary was Israel Yelin, who had succeeded David Applebaum as reader of the Newcastle synagogue in 1894 and who had subsequently moved to London. The seven *mohelim* engaged a Dr E. Q. Ambrose to provide them with a collective testimonial. In the letter he wrote, he stated that he had observed every one of the seven performing a circumcision and "had much pleasure in testifying to the ability displayed by each of them in its performance. The operation, as performed by the reverend gentlemen, did not take more than half a minute, and the antiseptic precautions were all that could be desired". Yelin arranged for Dr. Ambrose's testimonial to be published.[274]

There is good reason for suspecting that the London Association of Mohelim came about not only to establish or reinforce the credentials of its members as independent *mohelim*, separate from the Initiation Society, but also as a defensive measure to avoid action being taken against

272   *JW*, 30th January 1903, p.351.
273   *JC*, 27th February 1903, p. 16.
274   *JW*, 13th March 1903, p.461.

specific members. The letter's publication in March 1903 took place within a few weeks of two of the association's members being involved in inquests into the deaths of children they had lately circumcised. Both had been exonerated, but they must have felt, being outside the Initiation Society, somewhat exposed. Perhaps, too, the word had got out that Joseph Blank had supplied certain names to the Chief Rabbi.

The association seems to have been short-lived. The Chief Rabbi and the Initiation Society pressed ahead with reform. An advisory committee was constituted by the society to formulate new measures for the registration and instruction of *mohelim*. It reported in March 1903. The society should have a medical board, which, together with the medical officer, would oversee surgical matters. A register of *mohelim* authorised by the Chief Rabbi and the Initiation Society should be compiled and maintained and appearance of their names should be evidence of competency as to religious precepts as well as the requirements of modern surgery. To appear in the register, *mohelim* must undertake to observe the regulations of the society. The report also contained draft regulations as to the method of performing operations and a draft syllabus of instruction.

On 19th March, at the annual meeting of the Initiation Society, attended by, among others, the Chief Rabbi and Sir Samuel Montagu, the members adopted the recommendations of the report. In the course of the meeting, Louis Montagu, at his most robust, inveighed against one of the more persistent critics of the society, who was not present and whom he did not name, and, with the support of the Chief Rabbi, asked publicly that the critic cease corresponding with non-Jews on the issue of Jewish circumcision.[275]

---

275 *JC*, 27th March 1903 p.22. The unnamed critic was M. Russell Rubens. A persistent thorn in the side of the society, he attended the Israel Stavisky inquest on 1st February 1905 and attempted to harangue the court, but was slapped down by Wynne Baxter (J.Snowman to H.Adler, 1st February 1905, LMA ACC/2805/03/01/021).

The proposed new register did not satisfy critics.[276] It was observed that, given that the Initiation Society had no legal power to compel *mohelim* to register, there was no great difference between the old system and the new. Nevertheless, the Chief Rabbi and the Initiation Society persisted and in August 1903 a letter, signed by Adler and Louis Montagu [Appendix E] was despatched to *mohelim* not associated with the society, presumably those whose names and addresses had been obtained by Joseph Blank. They were informed about the new register, how widely it would be circulated, and the risks, not clearly specified, that *mohelim* were likely to face with the secular authorities if they experienced problems while remaining unregistered. They were therefore encouraged to come forward to register, with all that entailed.

Although the Initiation Society was, in strictly legal terms, a toothless beast, the efforts of Dr Adler and the society's leadership started to achieve results. In March 1904, it was being reported at the society's annual meeting that its medical board had enacted regulations for the teaching of non-medical *mohelim* who had prepared a register of all *mohelim* that had been taught and examined in the proper use of modern antiseptics.[277] A year later, it was reported that the register had been published, several *mohelim* had been re-examined and ten would-be *mohelim* had been instructed and were now registered.[278] The society also appointed a medical officer, Dr Jacob Snowman.

Snowman became a determined proponent of modernisation in the medical aspects of *bris millah* and in this he had the cautious support of the Chief Rabbi. Snowman was religiously observant, although, for some in the Initiation Society, he was not religious enough. He seems to have been criticised for minor lapses in observance and acknowledged

276   *JC*, 27th March 1903 p.22; *JW*, 21st August 1903, p.432.
277   *JC*, 11th March 1904, p.30.
278   *JC*, 5th May 1905, p.32.

that he occasionally carried an umbrella on the Sabbath.[279] He produced a readable, practical handbook for *mohelim,* available from the society for half a crown (12.5p),[280] but ran into trouble over a passage relating to *mezizah.*[281] With his appointment, the society entered into an activist phase, its secretary, medical officer and members of its medical board bringing to the attention of the Chief Rabbi cases of negligent performance of circumcisions by *mohelim* and requesting or supporting action by the *Beth Din.*[282]

279 J Snowman to H Adler, 13th September 1904, LMA ACC/2805/03/01/021.

280 Snowman, op.cit.

281 The ancient practice of *mezizah* requires suction by the mouth of the *mohel* on the wound. There had been discussion among orthodox British Jews as to whether this practice was still required by Jewish law (see, for example, letters to the *Jewish World,* 21st September 1894, p.2; 5th October 1894, p.6; 12th October 1894, p.2; and 2nd November 1894, p.2). The conservative view was that the requirement remained in full force. When Snowman came to write his handbook, his original comments on *mezizah* worried the Chief Rabbi. "I am certain that your observations as they stand will invoke an immense amount of hostile animadversions, and even prevent the general adoption of the book", he wrote (H.Adler to J.Snowman, 15th July 1904, LMA ACC/2805/03/01/021). Snowman and the society's medical board were opposed to the practice of *mezizah* except through a sterilised glass tube and wanted the *Beth Din* to come out clearly against the practice of direct suction. Adler pleaded with Snowman to go along with an ambiguous ruling from the *Beth Din.* He feared a split in the religious court if the society's medical board insisted on a clear statement declaring the practice of direct suction obsolete. Rabbi Chaikin, a religious conservative, had been brought into the *Beth Din* with difficulty and Adler did not want precarious communal unity to fracture, as it might do if Chaikin felt compelled to issue a minority ruling and declare publicly that he dissented from the *Beth Din's* ruling (H. Adler to J. Snowman, 5th January 1905, LMA ACC/2805/03/01/021). It is evident that Snowman and the medical board had Adler's sympathy, but, as far as Adler was concerned, there were bigger issues in play.

282 M. Abrahams to H. Adler, 2nd December 1904 (mohel – Lazarus Simmons); J. Snowman to H. Adler, 3rd February 1905 (*mohel* - Barnet Shyman [sic]); M. Clifford to H. Adler, 16th February 1905, (*mohel* – Walter Phillips); all LMA ACC/2805/03/01/021.

The United Synagogue movement, far more capable of being influenced by the Chief Rabbi than the Federation, was also mobilised to bring pressure on *mohelim*. Its council in 1904 adopted a bye-law requiring salaried officers to give the whole of their time to their synagogues, unless they had the leave of the council. This meant that any *chazan* who also a *mohel* could not perform circumcisions without permission and thereby gave the council the power to prevent *chazanim* who were not members of the Initiation Society from practising, unless they were prepared to lose their salaried employment.[283]

A more direct way in which a practising but unregistered *mohel* could be induced to be examined by the society and become registered and subject to its rules was the threat of being prohibited from practising by the *Beth Din,* a prohibition that would be publicised by a notice being placed in the Jewish press. There was a template for this kind of action. The Board for the Affairs of Schechita, which licensed kosher butchers, often placed "Notices to the Jewish Public" in the Jewish press informing readers that this or that butcher was not a licence-holder and that his meat and poultry was *treifah*. This type of regulatory action came to be used in relation to *mohelim*. There was of course no legal action that the Chief Rabbi and the *Beth Din* could take if a *mohel* defied a notice and continued to operate. However, the mere threat of prohibition and the publication of a notice might be sufficient to oblige a recalcitrant *mohel* to fall into line. Any *mohel* who felt he could continue in practice once a notice had been published would need to be supremely confident of the strength of his reputation.

Another source of pressure in forcing *mohelim* to submit to examination and registration was the way in which Wynne E Baxter, Coroner for East London, began to take a less patient line with *mohelim* and to treat

---

283   *JC*, 19th February 1904, p.18.

the Initiation Society as their regulator. Following the Finer case, there were several East End inquests in 1903-4 into deaths after circumcision. One, incredibly, again involved Simon Goldstein, who was somehow back in practice. Another was the Harris Prager case, involving David Applebaum. In none of these cases was any fault attributed to the *mohelim* concerned. However, in one of the inquests in June 1904,[284] Baxter observed that the issue of the competency of *mohelim* had "reached the ears of the Home Secretary" who, said Baxter, had specially requested coroners to investigate these cases carefully to establish whether there had been any negligence by *mohelim*. This may have been the reason why Baxter took a much tougher line in three infant death inquests in which he presided in the first half of 1905.

Israel, the son of Morris Stavisky, died a few days after circumcision in January 1905.[285] A London hospital doctor gave evidence that the death was due to exhaustion following gangrene and inflammation of the groin. The *mohel*, Barnett Scheinman, did not hold any certificate from the Initiation Society, a fact that went down badly with Baxter, who stated that it was his understanding that a *mohel* must have a certificate from "the Jewish board" and the Chief Rabbi. On examination by the coroner, it was clear that Scheinman did not know the difference between ordinary lint and anti-septic lint. In reply to similar questions he admitted ignorance. A juror referred to Scheinman as "a bungler". Baxter, in reviewing the facts, said that the *mohel* had no right to act as such. It was doubtful whether he had used any anti-septic measures at all. The jury brought in a "verdict of death by misadventure" and added that Scheinman should not carry out any further circumcisions without an Initiation Society certificate. Baxter called him forward and warned him that serious action would be taken if Scheinman came before him

---

284   *JC*, 1st July 1904, p.31.
285   *JC*, 3rd February 1905, p.14.

again in similar circumstances. Shortly afterwards, Scheinman was prohibited by the *Beth Din* from acting as a *mohel*.[286]

It is clear that by this stage a degree of cooperation had developed between London coroners and the Jewish authorities on the issue of negligent *mohelim*. The Chief Rabbi's office would be warned if and when an inquest was impending in which Jewish ritual circumcision was likely to be a factor. Thus, on 14th February 1905, the deputy coroner of Central London wrote to the Chief Rabbi to tell him that an inquest was due to take place the next day in St Pancras Coroner's Court relating to a child who had died the previous day. The *mohel* was Walter Phillips and the basic facts of the case were outlined in the deputy coroner's letter.[287]

On 12th May 1905, Baxter held an inquest into the death of Harris Poppick, the son of a tailor's machinist.[288] The child had been circumcised by a *mohel* called Lewis Cohen. About four hours after the *bris*, bleeding started, which Cohen stopped, but it started again the next day. A doctor was called, but the baby died. Cohen said he was a registered *mohel* with twenty-five years' experience who circumcised about a hundred children a year. The doctor deposed that there had been no clotting of the blood and the child had been insufficiently bandaged. He told the inquest that the seriousness of the case had not been appreciated by the *mohel*. It transpired that Cohen had never attended any Initiation Society training sessions. The coroner took the view that the *mohel* had done everything as far as his knowledge went, but this was a special case and the *mohel* had not understood it. "There was a society formed and a doctor appointed to instruct the *mohelim*, but a lot of them would not attend, as they thought they knew all about

---

286   *JC*, 10th February 1905, p.2. In the notice, his name was spelt as "Sheiman". The notice also prohibited Lazarus Simon from practising (see Appendix F).

287   W. Schroder to H. Adler, 14th February 1905, LMA ACC/2805/03/01/021. The inquest was not reported in the Jewish press.

288   *JC*, 19th May 1905, p.24.

the work", Baxter said. Several jurors remarked that although Cohen had shown lack of technical knowledge, there had not been any wilful neglect. Baxter called Cohen forward and told him that that if the jury had not taken a merciful view, Cohen might have been sent to the Old Bailey to be tried for manslaughter. He strongly advised Cohen to take a proper course of training with the society and obtain a certificate. The jury's finding was that "death was due to excessive haemorrhage consequent on circumcision, such death being due to misadventure".

Within ten days, Baxter was presiding over yet another inquest into death after circumcision.[289] Emanuel Harris, the son of a journeyman tailor, had been circumcised by Morris Baum. Bleeding had recommenced which the *mohel* had been unable to stop. A doctor had been called in, but he was unable to prevent the baby dying. Baum told the inquest that he had held a certificate from the Chief Rabbi for twenty-one years, which had been received after due examination. Further, he had carried out a number of circumcisions in the presence of Mr Abrahams of the Initiation Society, even though he was not a member of the society. He also produced a letter regarding his capabilities from Dr Ambrose, the provider of the testimonial for members of the London Association of Mohelim. The medical evidence given was that the circumcision had been expertly performed, but the *mohel* failed to appreciate that the case was out of the ordinary. Baum was recalled and sought to defend his conduct. Baxter criticised him for not getting a doctor involved in the case sooner. He also asked why Baum was not a member of the Initiation Society. Baum replied that he was an experienced *mohel* and that the young men at the society had nothing to teach him. Baxter responded: "That's what you say. Have they not Dr Snowman giving all his time to teach this business? In this case I must express my view that you have not risen to the occasion". As the hearing concluded, Baxter issued a general warning: "I have not looked on

289 *JC*, 26th May 1905, p.30.

these cases seriously, but I shall have to do so in the future, if we get any more of them. In this instance, the *mohel* has just saved himself by the skin of his teeth. If he had not had a doctor called in at all I should have advised the jury to return a verdict of manslaughter." He attributed blame to both Baum and the doctor who had first been called in to see the child. "This case must be a warning to *mohelim*", he sternly pronounced, "and I clearly give them to understand that if anything like this happens again I shall send the case to the Old Bailey, and they will be tried for manslaughter". The jury returned a verdict that "the child had died from haemorrhage after circumcision, and that the same was due to misadventure."

A *Jewish Chronicle* editorial soon after the inquest,[290] headed "A Warning to Mohelim", supported Baxter and urged every *mohel* in the country, who had not yet done so, to submit themselves to training by the Initiation Society. It also urged the Jewish community to select only *mohelim* who were on the Initiation Society's list. However, it went on, if a minority of Jews still refused to use only Initiation Society *mohelim*, and thereby jeopardised the Jewish community's good name, perhaps some form of legally compulsory registration should be welcomed. But no such regime of statutory regulation ensued. Instead, after 1905, inquest reports in the Jewish press on post-circumcision deaths cease to appear and, as far as a reader of the Edwardian Jewish press is concerned, the "Circumcision Scandal" comes, quite abruptly and perhaps surprisingly, to an end.

---

290   *JC*, 14th July 1905, p.8.

The author has located eleven coroners' inquests in London during 1902-5 into deaths after Jewish circumcision which were reported or referred to in the Jewish press and from which it is possible to identify the name of the dead child (Appendix C). The content of the earliest news reports strongly suggests that London coroners had not been involved to any great extent in inquests like these before 1902. After 1905, such news reports cease altogether, to the great relief of the leaders of the Jewish community. At the Initiation Society annual meeting in 1908,[291] *Dayan* Hyamson expressed pleasure that there had been no recurrence of the "epidemic of inquests that had created such scandal a few years ago." The Initiation Society, he said, instead of being a charitable organisation only, had also become an educational institution and a college for the training and inspection of *mohelim*. Among recent innovations was a system of periodic inspection of all *mohelim* by rotation. The society was, however, only able to make the change *Dayan* Hyamson described by moving a proportion of its slender resources away from providing financial benefits to poor parents, which payments were now reduced, to paying the salary of a medical officer.[292] Priorities had changed.

A driving force behind the transformation of the Initiation Society was the Chief Rabbi, Dr Hermann Adler. At the society's 1909 annual meeting, congratulations were proposed to him on the approaching 50th anniversary of his becoming a minister. Louis Montagu seconded the motion stating that Dr Adler had always been of great service to the society, but then, he added somewhat acerbically, their society had always been of service to Dr Adler.[293] It was, of course, Montagu who had for some years been the main financial support to the society. Communal laurels must, however,

---

291 *JC*, 14th February 1908, p.28.
292 Another new obligation which the Society had assumed since the beginning of the century and which required a diversion of its resources was the funding of nursing assistance. This was eventually arranged through the Sick Rooms Helps Society.
293 *JC*, 23rd April 1909, p. 18.

be shared between the Chief Rabbi and the medical board of the society. Board members were zealous in bringing to the Chief Rabbi's attention cases of alleged negligence by *mohelim* and in following up afterwards if action by the *Beth Din* was slow or unforthcoming.

The scale of the "Circumcision Scandal" problem is difficult to estimate. At its outset, critics of circumcision by medically unqualified *mohelim* were alleging that a large number of Jewish babies were dying unnecessarily. One letter to the *Jewish Chronicle* described it as a "massacre of the innocents".[294] But where were the data behind such hyperbole? Certainly, some individuals had suffered deaths in their families which they attributed to negligence by *mohelim*. But there was a degree of vagueness, a lack of specificity about names and dates and places, to back up expansive allegations and this made it easy for some, like Louis Montagu, in an outburst at an Initiation Society meeting in March 1903, to assert that there was no significant problem at all.[295] There is no doubt, however, on reading the 1900-1905 newspaper reports and letters from the society to the Chief Rabbi that there were *mohelim* in practice, perhaps only few in number, who were careless or ignorant or both - and who were therefore dangerous. It seems to have been relatively easy, however, either through fear of suspension by the *Beth Din* or by actual suspension and concomitant bad publicity, to compel these *mohelim* to re-train and be made subject to the Initiation Society's rules or be put out of business. This seems to be the only conclusion one can draw from the absence of cases reported or referred to in the Jewish press after 1905.[296]

---

294 *JC*, 23rd January 1903, p.8.

295 *JC*, 27th March 1903, p.22.

296 A qualification to this statement is that there is little information about the situation in the provinces. Correspondence between the Initiation Society and the Chief Rabbi in 1904-5 indicates that neither had much idea what was happening outside London and that regulating circumcision in the provinces was as yet beyond the society's reach (J. Snowman to H. Adler, 1st February 1905, LMA ACC/2805/03/01/021).

The British Medical Journal, in an article in March 1903,[297] described how the Initiation Society had recast its rules by establishing a supervisory medical board of registered surgeons. The *Journal* took the view that "it is evident that there is no valid reason for the outcry which has been raised in some quarters regarding what is called the reckless sacrifice of infant life. The Jewish Community is clearly quite alive to its responsibilities in this matter, and is prepared to remedy as far as possible the evil conditions which obtain in some cases. As far as the Initiation Society is concerned, the precautions proposed appear to be sufficient". This view of the capacity of the Jewish community to solve its own problems through its own institutions turned out to be correct. The leading forces in doing so were the Chief Rabbi and an activist Initiation Society medical board. Nevertheless, whether the results they achieved could have been attained so quickly and effectively without the back-up of dread warnings from the Coroner of East London is a matter of some doubt. While the *Beth Din* had the power to cause loss of reputation and livelihood to a negligent *mohel*, Wynne Baxter could have him sent to the Old Bailey.

---

297   *British Medical Journal*, 28th March 1903, p.748.

25. Another Death - and the Protection of Registration

On 23rd June 1905, the following notice appeared in the Jewish press:[298]

NOTICE TO THE JEWISH COMMUNITY.

NOTICE IS HEREBY GIVEN that MR DAVID APPLEBOAM of 149 , Whitechapel-road has been PROHIBITED by the Chief Rabbi and the Beth Din from acting as mohel [in Hebrew].
By order
M.ABRAHAMS
Secretary to the Initiation Society
London June 20th 1905 - 5665

An explanation of what had occurred is that, after the Harris Prager inquest, David Applebaum had been asked to attend a meeting of the medical board of the Initiation Society with a view to getting him examined as to his competence. Correspondence between the society and the Chief Rabbi evidences that even where a *mohel* had been exonerated by an inquest, this was not necessarily good enough for the society's medical board.[299] Either he did not attend before the medical board or he did so and then refused or failed to attend his examination. He probably did not cooperate with the society because he felt no obligation to do so. He did not belong to the society. He was an experienced *mohel* against whom no criticism had been levelled by the coroner. More than this, the coroner had gone out of his way to certify that the circumcision of Harris Prager had been "skilfully performed". Whatever his feelings in the matter, the society drew his non-cooperation to the attention of the *Beth Din*, which made a ruling prohibiting him from practising, and the notice was published. It brought him quickly to heel. Very soon after its publication, he submitted himself to examination by the society and, on 28th July 1905, a further notice appeared in the Jewish press:[300]

---

298   *JC*, 23rd June 1905, p.30; *JW,* 23rd June 1905, p.291.
299   E.g. Lazarus Simmons, Appendix F.
300   *JC*. 28th July 1905, p.2; *JW*, 28th July 1905, p.411.

INITIATION SOCIETY

NOTICE IS HEREBY GIVEN that MR DAVID APPELBOAM of 149 Whitechapel Road, having passed the Examination of the Medical Board of the Initiation Society, has been entered on the Register of Mohelim as qualified to perform the rite.
M.Abrahams
Secretary

Now possessing Initiation Society certification, David Applebaum became, for the last year-and-a half of his life, one of its authorised *mohelim*. As such, his name appears in the *Jewish Year Book* for 5667 (1906/7) and 5668 (1907/8). His registration seems to have protected him when, just four months after it had been obtained, he found himself before an inquest again after the death of another child he had circumcised.

In early November 1905, David Applebaum circumcised Charlie Rabinowitz, the son of Israel Rabinowitz, a Hebrew teacher. The Rabinowitz family lived in Old Montague Street, a few hundred yards from the Applebaum home. Israel Rabinowitz's occupation was lowly paid and it is a reasonable assumption that the family was poor, perhaps very poor. After the *bris* , the little boy haemorrhaged and on 4th November died, aged ten days old. Three days later an inquest took place at which Wynne Baxter presided. The inquest merited a brief report in the Jewish Chronicle.[301]

---

301 *JC*, 10th November 1905, p.35; report in full in Appendix B. The inquest was not reported in the *Jewish World*, the *East London Observer and Tower Hamlet and Borough of Hackney Chronicle* or the *Borough of Stepney and Poplar and East London Advertiser.*

Evidence was given to the inquest, presumably by a doctor who attended, that the *bris* had been properly performed, but the child had been suffering from jaundice. The coroner said that the evidence indicated that no one was to blame and a verdict of "death by misadventure" was returned. There was, however, an issue at the hearing as to whether David Applebaum should have gone ahead with the operation had he understood the seriousness of the child's condition. Baxter was displeased but was unable to criticise David Applebaum on the grounds that he was not registered with the Initiation Society. David Applebaum had, of course, only recently passed the society's examination and been registered and this made him immune from one of Baxter's usual fulminations. Baxter nevertheless remarked that the case was additional justification for circumcision only being conducted by a doctor. Had one been involved, he said, the baby's medical condition could have been detected.

But was this fair? The news report in the *Jewish Chronicle* is so brief that it is difficult to understand the medical facts of the case. Neonatal jaundice may stem from various physiological or pathological conditions, but the yellowish state which results is either readily apparent from the physical appearance of the child or in less obvious cases by the traditional test of blanching the skin with finger pressure to reveal the underlying colour of skin and subcutaneous tissue.[302] An experienced *mohel* of the time would not have missed a case of jaundice, even though he might not have fully understood its cause. Furthermore, he would have learned during his traditional apprenticeship that there is authority in the *Talmud* for deferring a child's circumcision until after the jaundice had passed.[303]

---

302   M. Jeffery Maisels, "Neonatal Jaundice", *Pediatrics in Review*, 2006; 27, 443-454, available on http://pedsinreview.aaplublications.org/cgi/content/full/27/12/442 (accessed 28th March 2013).

303   Whether the statement to this effect in the *Gemara, Shabbat* 134a, has the stature of Jewish law, is open to debate (Rabbi Joshua Flag, *Jaundice and Circumcision*, available on http://www.mohelinsouthflorida.com /2011/12/jaundice-when-baby-is-yellow.html, website of Rabbi Avi Billet (accessed 20th March 2013)).

Did David Applebaum fail to notice that the child had jaundice? Or was it readily apparent, but misinterpreted by him as a harmless form of physiological jaundice when it was in reality a serious pathological condition? And even had a doctor seen the child before the operation, given the state of medical science at the time, would he have better able than an experienced *mohel* to tell whether the child was healthy enough for circumcision? There is just not enough information in the news report to answer these questions adequately. It seems clear, though, that Baxter regarded David Applebaum less benignly now than he had done eighteen months before. His coroner's certificate, as transmitted to the registrar of the Mile End New Town registration sub-district, gives as cause of death: "Violent anoemia due to haemorrhage after circumcision favoured by jaundice." There is no statement that the circumcision had been "properly performed", as he had certified in the Harris Prager case.

David Applebaum practised as a *mohel* at a time in the East End when poverty, overcrowding and dirty living conditions increased the risk of the children of poor immigrant Jews suffering problems after circumcision. It was a high risk environment in which to work as a *mohel,* one in which more post-operative problems might be expected than in a practice among middle class West End Jews. Nevertheless, the thought nags at the mind of the author that perhaps the obverse of David Applebaum's easy-going, light-hearted attitude to life might have been a degree of casualness in his practice as a *mohel.* Eleven news reports of deaths of identifiable children after Jewish circumcision have been found during the period 1902-5 - and two of those were deaths in which David Applebaum was involved. It is a troubling statistic.

The circumstances of David Applebaum's death became part of family legend. In late January 1907, he performed a circumcision on a child whose identity we do not know. Reverend Applebaum probably already had the beginnings of a chest infection when he carried out the *bris*. Afterwards, he became quite ill and took to his bed, but then received a message that the child was haemorrhaging. He got up and went out to check on the baby. It was midwinter and an intense cold easterly wind had recently brought icy weather to Britain from the Continent. The child seems to have survived; certainly there is no press report from about this time of another East End death after circumcision. David Applebaum returned to his sick bed, but as a result of his visit, so the story goes, his health worsened and after five days of illness, on Saturday, 2nd February 1907, he died. His son, Maurice, was with him in his final hours. He was attended and his death certified by the same Dr Ambrose who had provided him and other members of the London Association of Mohelim with a written testimonial. The cause of death, given in the death certificate, was "Bronchitis & Emphysema Cardiac failure".

Emphysema is a lung disease which tends to get progressively worse. It is most often caused by smoking and exposure to air pollution. It would be surprising if David Applebaum had not smoked; most men of his time did. And the London air, with its pea-soup fogs, contributed to high levels of lung disease in the capital. He must have suffered from emphysema for some time and then developed a bronchial infection. Perhaps this had happened to him before. The infection would have left him desperately choking for breath and the great stress this caused to his heart led to cardiac arrest.

The Applebaum/Appleby family attributed his death to his selfless action in rising from his bed to tend to his infant patient. This was the legend that was passed down. Any knowledge of the deaths of the two babies,

Harris Prager and Charlie Rabinowitz, never became part of the family's collective memory. They were incidents in David Applebaum's life that seem never to have been recounted to younger members of the family.

Reverend Applebaum seems to have been a good natured and likeable man. It is perfectly credible, in risking his own health in order to visit a recently circumcised child, that his motivation was entirely unselfish. But he would not have been human if he had not also been propelled, and perhaps primarily so, by a strong desire for self-preservation. He had been twice in front of the coroner after a child he had circumcised had died. He must have known of Baxter's threat to send the next negligent *mohel* who came before him to the Old Bailey. He had also previously been in trouble with the Beth Din and had been prohibited from acting as a *mohel,* something which he must have feared could happen again. These considerations must have passed through his mind when he dragged himself out of bed, wheezing for breath, on a cold day in January 1907.

There were many visits and telegrams and letters of sympathy and condolence to the widow and family and the traditional one-week *shivah* (period of mourning) was duly held.[304] When it was over, and the low chairs were removed and the mirrors turned around, the family faced the inevitable economic consequences of the death of their principal *broitgeber* ("bread winner", Yiddish). David Applebaum had little in the way of savings. He certainly left no will that required proving and there was no grant of letters of administration. Four years later, the 1911 census reveals that two of his unmarried daughters were now going out to work, Annie as a cigarette packer and Rebecca as a tailoress. His widow, despite her reduced circumstances, cherished his memory and spoke uncritically and lovingly of him until her death thirty years later.

---

304   *JC,* 15th February 1907, p.2.

She refused to remove his professional brass plaque from beside the front door until she left 149 Whitechapel Road, a few years afterwards, to move to a new home a hundred yards away and where she was to live for the rest of her life. His sons and daughters remained fiercely proud of their father's memory and a large framed photograph [illustration B] hung on the wall of the North London house, where the author was brought up, until the 1970s. David Applebaum is buried in Plashet Cemetery in East Ham. The district has very few Jews living in it now and the cemetery gates are kept locked as a security precaution. On 6th May 2003, many of the gravestones in the cemetery were vandalised, but David Applebaum's [Illustration I] survived intact.

After David Applebaum's death, his eldest son Maurice took over as head of the family. But he lived some distance away from Whitechapel and had children of his own together with business and communal responsibilities. The younger Applebaum brothers had no father in the house to discipline or guide them and they started to run wild. But that is another story.

Acknowledgements

When I started researching my grandfather's life, I planned on producing something which would be of interest to his descendants. I also hoped that a properly footnoted life story would be of use to academic researchers working on such aspects of British Jewish history as the working lives of immigrant *chazanim*, the Jewish friendly society movement and the history of Newcastle Jewry and the East End *chevrot*. At the very least, I thought, it would be something for students and academics to quarry. It was a surprise, then, and a bonus for me, to stumble upon the Edwardian "Circumcision Scandal", an episode in British Jewish history which does not seem to have described before. Something else which I did not anticipate was how long it would take me complete the exercise. The cause of the delay was not any loss of interest, but the demands of working for an international oil company. Eventually, I was able to pick up my notebooks, compiled in the late 1980s, and carry on at the points where I left off. Doing so did not feel odd, but it was frustrating. Some interviewees had died and lines of enquiry which could have been followed while people were alive were now impossible to pursue. I particularly regret not having kept up correspondence after 1989 with a distant (half) cousin, Karl Applebaum, then a sick man living in retirement just outside New Orleans.

One person who, thankfully, is still with us is my mother, Elfrida Ruth Fine, who so helpfully remembered many bits of information that my late father, her much older first husband, told her about his family and childhood. Other family or relatives whose help I must gratefully acknowledge include Brian Appleby, Basil Appleby, Paul Appleby, Minnie Stein, Karl Applebaum, Irene Osgood, Harry Pavion, Lily Davidson, Ronald Shenker and Ninette Appleby. Assistance was also received from Walter Sharmer, archivist of the Newcastle Synagogue, Dr Morris Sifman and Maurice Levenson of the Initiation Society, Dr Rivkah Zim, Judith Bernstein, Dr David Zuck, Julian Preisler, David Bender, Professor

Michael Berkowitz, Dr Fay Bussgang, Michael Jolles, Dr Gabriel Sivan, Judith Samson, Lisa Penfold and Shirley Saunders. Thanks are also due to the Federation of Synagogues and the Office of the Chief Rabbi, each of which permitted me access to their Edwardian records. I must also express my gratitude to the staff of the *Jewish Chronicle* library in 1986-7, whose names I do not remember and most of who must by now be retired, for permitting me with the minimum of fuss to come in almost every day to use their library. Thanks are also due to my daughter, Bea Appleby, who designed the book cover. And, finally, I must thank my wife, Professor Dame Hazel Genn, for patiently and helpfully reading and commenting on successive drafts of this "Life" – some drafts almost identical to the drafts she had already reviewed – and for her greatly appreciated work in the production and layout of the final text.

Attentive readers of this life of David Applebaum will be well aware of the extent to which source material, or rather the absence of it, has shaped the narrative. In some areas, for example the upbringing of his daughters, nothing has been discovered and not much can be said. In other areas, where some piece of information is known, readers will have noted that the narrative may veer off in an unexpected direction. The author has done his best with what is available.

Even normally helpful primary written sources have their limitations. Registers of Births, Deaths and Marriages are full of useful data; however, they are not always comprehensive or accurate. We have seen that the birth of Hyman Applebaum was never registered and that of Manny Applebaum was registered as having taken place several hundred miles from where it actually occurred. Census returns are usually an excellent source of data and are easily available from Ancestry.co.uk. Nevertheless, in the course of research, it was discovered that there is a gap in the 1881 East End material available in the electronic database. Wilkes Street and some neighbouring streets are missing. Further enquiry to the National Archives revealed that although Wilkes Street appears in the 1871 and 1891 census returns, it does not appear among the 1881 returns. The most likely explanation, according to the National Archives's reader advice service, is that no census returns were ever completed for these streets. It was the practice at the time not to employ enumerators who lived in the areas they were enumerating. One imagines there could be several good reasons for this, including the need to preserve the confidentiality of census returns. However, this also means that enumerators did not know their designated districts well and left out streets in error. The mysterious omission of Wilkes Street is an unfortunate blank spot. If data were available, it is quite possible that we might discover that the Applebaum family were still in Spitalfields in the spring of 1881 and find out more about their household.

Some primary resources have suffered as a result of Second World War bombing. The records of the Initiation Society and the *Jewish Chronicle*'s files were destroyed in the Blitz. There are no records available of London Eastern District coroners' courts' proceedings before 1925. No records seem to have survived of the Fashion Street, Great Alie Street and St Mary Street synagogues for the periods in which David Applebaum worked for these congregations during 1895-1907. In contrast, the records of Jewish congregations in the North-East, as held by Tyne & Wear Archives in Newcastle, include a few pages of Newcastle synagogue ledgers from the early 1890s that contain accounting entries relating to him and which are the only contemporaneous synagogue records so far located anywhere relating to his employment as a clergyman.

The records of the Federation of Synagogues, as deposited with the London Metropolitan Archives and the University of Southampton, particularly the Federation's minutes and the letterbooks kept by its secretary, Joseph Blank, provide information about many East End *chevrot* that were Federation members. They do not, however, provide enough information about synagogues in Fashion Street or St Mary Street to enable accurate and complete histories of each to be written, even with the assistance of intermittent mentions in the Jewish press. The London Metropolitan Archives also hold the records of the Office of the Chief Rabbi during the rabbinate of Dr Hermann Adler. The letterbooks for the period are a challenge to any researcher and the author found them illegible. However, among these archives is a slim file on *Mezizah* in which some items of 1904-5 correspondence on negligent *mohelim* has been deposited. These illuminate the relationship between Adler and the society and reveal how activist its medical board became.

Much reliance has been placed on information from the English language Jewish press. The *Jewish Chronicle* and *Jewish World* are each a mine of information, but which nevertheless should be treated with a little caution as to their accuracy. We have seen how the two newspapers conflicted in 1898 when they each reported David Applebaum taking Passover services at a different synagogue. Family historians are also cautioned against over-reliance on electronic searches of the *Jewish Chronicle* archives. In the 1980s, the author read the *Jewish Chronicle* in hard copy for the period 1882-1907, electronic searches not being yet available. Numerous references to David Applebaum were noted which do not turn up in electronic searches. Conversely, electronic searches have located references which the author missed when he read the hard copies. A family historian making use of the *Jewish Chronicle* for the purposes of research needs therefore to do both; electronic searches and page turning/microfiche scrolling.

Turning to secondary sources, a list of books and articles which were of assistance is set out below.

Alderman G.(ed.), *Modern British Jewry*, Clarendon Press, Oxford, 1992.

Alderman G., *The Federation of Synagogues 1887-1987*, Federation of Synagogues, London, 1987.

Alderman G., *London Jewry and London Politics 1889-1986*, Routledge, London and New York, 1989.

Alderman G., *Controversy and Crisis; Studies in the History of Jews in Modern Britain*, Academic Studies Press, Boston, 2008.

Apple R., *Herman Gollancz & the title of rabbi in British Jewry*, presentation to the Jewish Historical Society of England Israel Branch, 30th May 2010, www.ozrorah.com/2010/06/herman-gollancz-the-title-of-rabbi-in-british-jewry/(accessed 9th March 2012).

Aronson I.M., "The Anti-Jewish Pogroms in Russia in 1881", in Klier and Lambroza (eds.), 1992.

Bailey P. (ed.), *Music Hall: The Business of Pleasure*, Open University Press, Milton Keynes and Philadelphia, 1986.

Barnavi E. (ed.), *A Historical Atlas of the Jewish People; from the Time of the Patriachs to the Present*, Hutchinson, London, 1992.

Berman R.L., *A House of David in the Land of Jesus*, Robert Lewis Berman, USA, 2007.

Bermant C., *The Cousinhood; the Anglo-Jewish Gentry*, Eyre & Spottiswoode, London, 1971.

Black E.C., *The Social Politics of Anglo-Jewry 1880-1920*, Basil Blackwell, Oxford, 1988.

Black G., *Jewish London; An Illustrated History*, Breedon Books, Derby, 2007 (first published 2003).

Cesarani D. (ed.),*The Making of Modern Anglo-Jewry,* Basil Blackwell, Oxford, 1990.

Cesarani D., *The Jewish Chronicle and Anglo-Jewry 1841-1991*, Cambridge University Press, Cambridge, 1994.

Dubnow S.M., *History of the Jews in Russia and Poland*, Jewish Publication Society of America, 1918 (reprinted by Filiquarian Publishing).

Eliach Y., *Once There Was A World; a 900-Year Chronicle of the Shtetl of Eishyshok*, Little, Brown and Company, Boston, New York and London, 1998.

Endelman T.M., *The Jews of Britain 1656-2000*, University of California Press, Berkeley, Los Angeles and London, 2002.

Feldman D., *Englishmen and Jews: Social Relations and Political Culture 1840-1914*, Yale University Press, New Haven and London, 1994.

Finestein I., *Jewish Society in Victorian England; Collected Essays*, Valentine Mitchell, London 1993.

Fishman W.J., *East End 1888: A year in a London borough among the labouring poor*, Gerald Duckworth, London , 1988.

Flag J., *Jaundice and Circumcision,* http:/www.mohelinsouthflorida.com/2011/12/jaundice-when-a-baby-is-yellow.html, website of Rabbi Avi Billet (accessed 21st March 2013).

Freedman M., *Leeds Jewry – The First Hundred Years*, Leeds Branch of the Jewish Historical Society of England, York, 1992.

Gairdner D., "The Fate of the Foreskin"; A Study of Circumcision", *British Medical Journal*, Vol 2, 24th December 1949.

Gartner L.P., *The Jewish Immigrant in England 1870-1914*, 3rd ed., Valentine Mitchell, London and Portland, Oregon, 2001 (first published 1960).

Gilbert M., *Atlas of Russian History*, Dorset Press, USA, 1972.

Glasman G., *East End Synagogues*, Museum of the Jewish East End, London, 1987.

Gordon W.J., "The Cleansing of London", http://www.victorianlondon. org/health/disposal.htm , originally published in *Leisure Hour*, 1889 (accessed 28th May 2012).

Holmes C., *Anti-Semitism in British Society 1876-1939*, Holmes & Meier Publishers Inc, New York, 1979.

Johnson P., *A History of the Jews*, Weidenfeld and Nicholson, London 1987.

Julius A., *Trials of the Diaspora; a History of Anti-Semitism in England*, Oxford University Press, Oxford, 2010.

Kersten A., "Yiddish as a Vehicle for Anglicization", on Klier and Lomborza, 1996.

Klier J.D., " Emigration Mania in Late Imperial Russia: Legend and Reality" in *Patterns of Migration 1850-1914*, Proceedings of the International Academic Conference of the Jewish Historical Society of England and the Institute of Jewish Studies, University College London, Newman N. and Massil S.W. (eds.), Jewish Historical Society of England and the Institute of Jewish Studies, University College London, London, 1996.

Klier J.D. and Lambroza S. (eds.), *Pogroms: Anti-Jewish Violence in Modern Russian History*, Cambridge University Press, Cambridge, 1992.

Krausz E., *Leeds Jewry: its History and Social Structure*, Heffer & Sons, Cambridge, 1964.

Kriwaczek P., *Yiddish Civilisation; The Rise and Fall of a Forgotten Nation*, Phoenix, London 2006 (first published by Weidenfeld & Nicolson, 2005).

Leigh G., *From Kretinga to Sunderland: a Jewish Chain Migration from Lithuania – Cause and Effect 1850-1930*, M.A.thesis, University of Newcastle – Department of History 2002 (unpublished).

Levy A., *History of the Sunderland Jewish Community 1755-1955*, Macdonald, London 1956.

Louvish S., *Chaplin: The Tramp's Odyssey*, Faber & Faber, London, 2009.

Maisels M.J., "Neonatal Jaundice", *Pediatrics in Review*, Vol 27, 2006.

Melnick S.C., *A Giant Among Giants*, Pentland Press, Durham, 1994.

Newman, A. (ed.), *The Jewish East End 1840 -1939*, Jewish Historical Society of England, London, 1981.

Olsover L., *The Jewish Communities of North-East England 1755-1980*, Ashley Mark, Gateshead, 1980.

Orbach A., "The Development of the Russian Jewish Community 1881-1903" in Klier and Lambroza (eds.), 1992.

Pasternak V., *The Jewish Music Companion*, Tara Publications, USA, 2002.

Petrovsky-Shtern Y., *Jews in the Russian Army 1827-1917; Drafted into Modernity*, Cambridge University Press, New York, 2009.

Preisler J., *Memorial to the Destroyed Jewish Community of Dobrzyn nad Wisla, Poland*, www.jpreisler.com/dobrzyn (accessed 27th September 2011).

Renton P., *The Lost Synagogues of London*, Tymsder Publishing, London 2000.

Rogger H., *Jewish Policies and Right-Wing Politics in Imperial Russia*, Macmillan, Oxford, 1986.

Rogger H., "The Pogrom Paradigm in Russian History" in Klier and Lamroza (eds.), 1992.

Rosebury A., "The Jewish Friendly Societies; a critical survey", *Jewish Chronicle*, 8th September 1905.

Russell D., *Popular Music in England 1840-1914; A Social History*, 2nd ed., Manchester University Press, Manchester & New York, 1997.

Rutherford L., "Managers in a Small Way: The Professionalism of Variety Artistes 1860-1914", in Bailey (ed.), 1986.

Samson J., "A Peek into the Polish Past", *Shemot*, Vol.,8,4, December 2002.

Seligman J., *Sunderland – A Litvak Community in North East England*, www.seligman.org.il/sunderland_jews.html (accessed 6th August 2012).

Sivan G.A., "They Sailed West; a Family Chronicle", *Shemot,* Vol. 10,3, September 2002.

Snowman J., *The Surgery of Ritual Circumcision*, Initiation Society, 1904.

Spector S. (gen. ed.), *The Encyclopedia of Jewish Life Before and During the Holocaust*, NYU Press, Jerusalem and New York, 2001.

Zangwill I., *Children of the Ghetto; A Study of a Peculiar People*, 3rd edition, William Heinemann, London, 1922 (first published 1892).

Zivotofsky A.Z., *What's the Truth about ...Kosher Soap,* www.oukosher. org/.../whats_ the_truth_aboutkosher_soap (accessed 14th September 2011).

Zuck D., "Mr Troutbeck as the Surgeon's Friend: The Coroner and the Doctors – an Edwardian Comedy", *Medical History,* 39, 1995.

A brief and preliminary version of this work, Appleby D., "Reverend Applebaum's Mercy Dash", appeared in *Shemot,* Vol 19, 3, December 2011.

APPENDICES

Appendex A: The Applebaum Children

The children of David and Jeanette Applebaum who grew to adulthood are listed below. A total of fourteen children were born alive (based on details provided for the 1911 census). Two died while babies or children. Their names and dates of birth/death are unknown. Stage names, where known, are in inverted commas. Dates stated to be "circa" are the author's best guess.

1. Maurice b circa 1875 - d 1963
2. Israel/Isidore b 1878 - d 1946
3. Hyman b circa 1880 - d 1957
4. Rose b circa 1883 - d 1959
5. Sarah b circa 1884 - d 1944
6. Annie b circa 1885 - d 1979
7. Samuel b 1887 - d 1963
8. Mark/"Syd Kirby" b 1889 - d 1923
9. Harry b 1891 - d 1980
10. Rebecca/Peggy b 1893 - d 1941
11. Manny/"Billie Harlem" b 1895 - d 1971
12. Lazarus/Leonard b 1897 - d 1978

1. INQUEST ON HARRIS PRAGER
News Report, *Jewish Chronicle*, 22nd April 1904, p.17.

Death after Circumcision – On Thursday week, Mr Wynne E Baxter, the East London Coroner, held an inquest at the Stepney Borough Coroner's Court, with reference to the death of Harris Prager, aged twelve days, the child of a cap maker, residing at 14, Leopold Street, Mile End, who died after circumcision. Barnett Prager, the father, deposed that the deceased was circumcised by the Rev. D. Appelbaum, a Mohel, on Thursday evening 17th [sic] inst. After the operation there was excessive haemorrhage which the Mohel was unable to stop. Witness called in Dr. Black, who attended several times until death which took place on the 12th. Jane Davis, residing at 102, Turners Road, Mile End Old Town, stated that she went out nursing and attended the mother of the deceased. After the circumcision, the deceased cried very much. Dr. Black stopped the bleeding for a time, but it started again on the Saturday and the child died on Tuesday. By the Coroner: After the circumcision the dressings were not interfered with in any way. David Appelbaum, residing at 149, Whitechapel Road, said he was a certificated Mohel, and performed the operation on the deceased which was carried out with all due care. He had been a Mohel for twenty-two years and had performed 9,000 operations without having any trouble before. Dr. George Black, of 230, Burdett Road, deposed to being called and finding great difficulty in stopping the bleeding. Death was due to syncope from loss of blood consequent on circumcision. The Coroner: Was there any want of skill on the part of the Mohel? Witness: I think the operation was perfectly well done. In my opinion the deceased was a haemopholic subject. The Coroner remarked that the child did not die a natural death; the circumcision was a religious rite which had to be performed and it was clear that the Mohel was an experienced official and duly qualified. The jury returned a verdict of "death by misadventure."

2. INQUEST ON CHARLIE RABINOWITZ
News Report, *Jewish Chronicle*, 10th November 1905, p.35.

Death after Circumcision – Mr Wynne E Baxter held an inquiry on Tuesday into the death of C. Rabinowitz, aged ten days (the son of Israel Rabinowitz, a Hebrew teacher of 109, Old Montague Street), who died from haemorrhage after circumcision. The mohel was Mr Appelbaum. Evidence was given to the effect that the operation was properly performed, but that the deceased was suffering at the time from jaundice. The Coroner said he did not see that the evidence showed there was any blame to be attached to anyone in the case, but it furnished additional justification for the operation being performed by a medical man, who would have detected the disease. A verdict of "death from misadventure" was returned.

Appendex C: Jewish Circumcision Deaths in London 1902-05

The following is a list of identifiable boy babies who died after circumcision (although not necessarily as a result of the operation) and whose deaths were subject to a coroner's inquest reported by the Jewish press or reported elsewhere and referred to in the Jewish press:

1. LIPMAN FISHER

Report: *Evening Standard*, 1ˢᵗ February 1902, p.1.

Mohel: Simon Goldstein
Coroner: Wynne E Baxter

Cause of death: haemorrhage, perhaps some consequence of the manner of cutting.
Culpability: *mohel* criticised by coroner for not calling a doctor as soon as problems arose.

2. MICHAEL DOSTENOK/ PASDENOCK

Report: *Jewish World*, 2ⁿᵈ January 1903, p.272 and 9ᵗʰ January 1903, pp.288-9.

Mohel: Simon Goldstein
Coroner: John Troutbeck

Cause of death: septic poisoning.
Culpability: *mohel* criticised by the coroner for "the looseness of his arrangements" and a lack of proper understanding of anti-septic methods in modern surgery. Criticism also levelled at the Initiation Society for licensing the *mohel* to operate again after his previous suspension without "great precautions".

3. MARX GRIPPER

Report: *Jewish World*, 30th January 1903, p.351.

Mohel: Mr Ebbitz, assistant to Reverend Isaac Yelin.
Coroner: Dr E. King Honchin

Cause of death: blood poisoning from dirt in wound.
Culpability: no criticism of *mohel*.

4. [NO FIRST NAME] FINER

Report: *Jewish Chronicle*, 27th February 1903, p.16.

Mohel: Israel Woolf
Coroner: Wynne E. Baxter

Cause of death: death found to be unconnected with circumcision.
Culpability: no criticism of *mohel*.

5. SAMUEL BENJAMIN

Report: *Jewish Chronicle*, 25th September 1903, p.26.

Mohel: Simon Goldstein
Coroner: Wynne E. Baxter

Cause of death: septic poisoning.
Culpability: no criticism of *mohel*.

6. HARRIS PRAGER (see Appendix B)
Report: *Jewish Chronicle*, 22nd April 1904, p.17.

Mohel: David Applebaum
Coroner: Wynne E. Baxter

Cause of death: haemophilia.
Culpability: no criticism of *mohel*.

7. JACOB SCHWARZ
Report: *Jewish Chronicle*, 1st July 1904, p.31.

Mohel: Joshua Simons
Coroner: Wynne E Baxter

Cause of death: haemorrhage.
Culpability: no criticism of *mohel*.

8. ISRAEL STAVISKY
Report: *Jewish Chronicle*, 3rd February 1905, p.14.

Mohel: Barnet Marcus Scheinman
Coroner: Wynne E. Baxter

Cause of death: exhaustion following gangrene and inflammation
                    of the groin.
Culpability: *mohel* criticised for not possessing a certificate from
                    the Initiation Society. Coroner doubted whether *mohel*
                    had used any anti-septic measures at all. *Mohel* warned
                    that if he performed a circumcision again without an
                    Initiation Society certificate there would be a criminal
                    prosecution.

9. HARRIS POPPICK

Report: *Jewish Chronicle* 19ᵗʰ May 1905, p.24; also,
           British Medical Journal, 10th June 1905, p.1307.

Mohel: Lewis Cohen
Coroner: Wynne E. Baxter

Cause of death: haemorrhage
Culpability: *mohel* criticised for lack of technical knowledge and for
                not having obtained an Initiation Society certificate.

10. EMANUEL HARRIS

Report: *Jewish Chronicle,* 26ᵗʰ May 1905, p.30; also
           The Lancet, 10ᵗʰ June 1905, p1593.

Mohel: Morris Baum
Coroner: Wynne E. Baxter

Cause of death: haemorrhage.
Culpability: *mohel* criticised by the coroner for not having called
                in a doctor early enough and for not being a member
                of the Initiation Society. A doctor involved in the case
                was also criticised by the coroner.

11. CHARLIE RABINOWITZ (see Appendix B)
Report: Jewish Chronicle, 10ᵗʰ November 1905, p.35.

Mohel: David Applebaum
Coroner: Wynne E. Baxter

Cause of death: haemorrhage.
Culpability: no criticism of the mode of operation, although coroner
                 remarked that the circumstances of the case furnished
                 additional justification for circumcisions only being
                 conducted by doctors.

Two deaths after circumcision figure in correspondence between the Initiation Society and the Chief Rabbi in 1904-5. In both cases, the society's medical board blamed the *mohel,* attributed the children's deaths to the application of undiluted or insufficiently diluted carbolic acid, and sought action (M. Abrahams to H. Adler 2nd December 1904 and 5ᵗʰ February 1905; J.Snowman to H. Adler 15ᵗʰ February 1905 and 28ᵗʰ February 1905; all correspondence - LMA ACC/2805/03/01/021). The *mohelim* concerned are named in correspondence as Lazarus Simmons and Walter Phillips. It is not clear whether the case in which Simmons was involved was the Jacob Schwarz case (Appendix C) or another case altogether. The case involving Phillips was not reported in the Jewish press.

Appendix D - The Chief Rabbi's Letter to the Federation

Letter dated 13th February 1902 from Chief Rabbi, Hermann Adler, to Joseph Blank, secretary of Federation of Synagogues, as published in the *Jewish World*, 18th June 1902, p.330:

Dear Mr Blank,

I must beg you to bring the following important matter under the notice of the Federation.

I was deeply grieved by reading in the Evening Standard of 1st Inst the account of an inquest on a child that had died after the operation of Milah *[in Hebrew script] by Simon Goldstein of Chicksand Street. I cannot say how far the opinion mentioned at the inquest is correct, that the child's death was due to a lack of skill on the part of the operator. I felt it my duty to suspend Mr Goldstein forthwith, until he had been tested by the Surgeon* Mohel *appointed by the Initiation Society [full Hebrew name in Hebrew script] as to his competency.*

I have not yet heard that he has submitted himself to this examination.

This regrettable incident opens up a wide question. There are at present a great number of mohelim *[in Hebrew script] who have not been authorised by the society or by myself to act in this capacity. It is universally acknowledged that the operation is a very simple one and absolutely free from danger. Day after day the sanitary value of the sacred rite is more fully acknowledged by the most eminent medical and surgical authorities. But the operation is not without peril if performed without due regard to cleanliness and the precautions taught by medical science. I therefore deem it of great importance that the* mohelim *[in Hebrew script] of the metropolis, other than those authorised by me, should also be taught these rules and also submit to an examination by the officer of the Society. I would beg the members of the Federation to assist us in this object by furnishing me with the names and addresses of all the* mohelim [in Hebrew script] *practising in the East End and other districts. I will then endeavour to induce the Society to have these* mohelim [in Hebrew script] *examined and to publish the names of those who have satisfactorily passed the examination.*

I feel confident that I may reckon upon the cooperation of all your members in this sacred and important object.

Letter signed by the Chief Rabbi, Dr Hermann Adler, and the president of the Initiation Society, Louis Montagu, "circulated among those concerned", as the text appeared in the *Jewish World*, 14th August 1903, p.420:

Dear Sir,

In consequence of certain incidents which have occurred in connection with Milah [in Hebrew] *the Committee of the Initiation Society, acting in concert with the Ecclesiastical Authorities, have determined to take such steps as they hope may, with Divine help, prevent similar occurrences in the future. With that object in view, these two bodies have decided to introduce an official register of the names and addresses of all persons in the United Kingdom and British Colonies who are fully qualified to perform* Milah [in Hebrew], *and after completion of such register only those persons who are registered will be authorised to perform the ceremony. The Register, as soon as it is completed, will be sent to the Synagogues, Chevras, etc., due publicity will be given to among our co-religionists and copies will be forwarded to Parish Clerks and other local authorities, every possible endeavour being made to induce the Jewish Community throughout the United Kingdom and Colonies to enlist the services of registered mohelim and no others.*

We think it right to add that any persons hereafter acting as Mohel, without having been entered on the Register, must accept the responsibility of such action, especially under certain contingencies; in the event of actions [in Hebrew, actual word unclear] *possibly rendering himself liable to criminal proceedings.*

We feel assured that you are as anxious as we that the sacred rite should be performed in accordance with the mandate of our Holy Faith and, therefore, beg you to communicate at once with the Secretary of the

Initiation Society, Mr M Abrahams, 4 Beresford Terrace, Highbury New Park, who will acquaint you with the steps to be taken with a view to be placed on the Register. There is no charge for registration.

Appendix F - London *Mohelim* not associated
with the Initiation Society 1903

JOSEPH BLANK LIST

Below are the names and addresses stated in the list furnished by the secretary of the Federation to the Chief Rabbi, under cover of the secretary's letter dated 19ᵗʰ January 1903, and sent in belated response to the Chief Rabbi's letter of 13ᵗʰ February 1902.

Mr D Applebaum	*75 Whitechapel St*
Mr S Goldstein	*41 Chicksand St*
Rev M Epstein	*New Synagogue*
" *A E Gordon*	*2 Prescott St*
" *J Woolf*	*66 Sidney St*
" *P Fassenfeld*	*163 Commercial Road*
" *Dancyger*	*35 Scarborough St*
" *Ostroff*	*37* "
" *M Claff*	*31 Sidney St, Mile End*
" *I Yelin*	*9 Princelet St*
" *Symonds*	*4 Chicksand St*
" *Rosen*	*9 Fourth Avenue, Manor Park*

LONDON ASSOCIATION OF MOHELIM

Below are the members of the association as their names are stated in the testimonial letter provided by Dr E Q Ambrose and published in the *Jewish World* (13ᵗʰ March 1903, p.461).

The Reverend A Tertis
The Reverend I H Yellin
The Reverend L Goldstein
The Reverend S Applebaum
The Reverend L Wolf
The Reverend M Ebitz
The Reverend T Ostroff.

There are at least two errors in Dr Ambrose's testimonial which were not corrected, presumably because there was a wish to get the letter out to the Jewish press as fast as possible, rather than send it back to Dr Ambrose for correction. Reverend Yelin was by this time spelling his name with a single 'l', and this is how it is spelt in his covering letter; however, in the letter from Dr Ambrose he enclosed, the name is spelled "Yellin". "S Applebaum" is undoubtedly David Applebaum.

INDIVIDUAL MOHELIM

The London Association of Mohelim was prepared to style David Applebaum "Reverend", but Joseph Blank was not. One reason for this may be that in January 1903 David Applebaum had left the employ of Great Alie Street Synagogue and had not yet obtained a position with another synagogue.

"Mr S Goldstein", as identified in the Joseph Blank list, was the *mohel* of that name who was involved in the Lipman Fisher inquest in January 1902, the Michael Dostenok/Pasdenock inquest of January 1903 and the Samuel Benjamin inquest of September 1903 (Appendix C). He may be the same person as "The Reverend L Goldstein", who was a member of the London Association of Mohelim.

"Reverend J Woolf", as mentioned in the Joseph Blank List, and "Reverend L Wolf", as identified Dr Ambrose's testimonial, are believed to be the same person as "Israel Woolf", who had been involved in the Finer inquest in February 1903 (Appendix C). Among the archives of the Office of the Chief Rabbi (LMA ACC/2805/03/01/021) there is a small promotional postcard produced by "J Woolf, Plotzkar Specialist Mohel". Persons requiring his services were invited to stamp the postcard with a half-penny stamp and post it to him with their names and address on the reverse. The card had been sent to the Initiation Society by a Mr Samuel of Clapton with an enquiry as to whether Mr Woolf was an Initiation Society certified *mohel*, which he was not.

"Reverend M Ebitz" was Reverend Yelin's assistant, who had been involved in the Max Gripper inquest in January 1903 (Appendix C).

Reverend Ostroff was a London-based *chazan* (*JC*, 14th October 1904, p.8).

"Reverend Symonds" is probably the same person as the "Joshua Simons" who was a *mohel* in the Jacob Schwarz case in June 1904 (Appendix C) and the "Lazarus Simmons", who was the subject of correspondence between the Initiation Society and the Chief Rabbi in 1904-5. A child had died after circumcision and, at the ensuing inquest, Lazarus Simmons had perjured himself, so the secretary of the society alleged. It was "a worse case than of Scheinman", the secretary told Adler. Simmons had failed to attend before the society's medical board and the secretary reported the case to the *Beth Din* and requested action be taken (M.Abrahams to H.Adler 2nd December 1904, 5th February 1905; LMA ACC/2805/03/01/021). The *Beth Din* duly ruled against him and he was prohibited from practising (*JC*, 10th February 1905, p.2).

The leading light of the London Association of Mohelim seems to have been Reverend Yelin, its secretary, who wrote at least twice to the Jewish press on its behalf. Its most senior and well-known figure, however, would have been Reverend Tertis. In an 1886 advertisement (e.g. *JW*, 15th January 1886, p.5), he claimed to have practised as a *mohel* for eleven years. He came to London to become reader of the Princes Street Synagogue in 1878, a post he filled until 1887 (Melnick, op.cit, pp.48-52). He left, it appears, to concentrate on being a full-time *mohel*. He prospered and was later able to move from the East End to upmarket Stamford Hill. He took his profession seriously and in 1905 published an article in the *Lancet* on a new surgical dressing to be used after Jewish circumcision (*JC*, 8th December 1905, p.31). His name is not mentioned in the Joseph Blank list, which is surprising given that he was a well- known figure who had advertised his services in the Jewish press for many years. It is possible that he had made his own special arrangement with the Initiation Society.

A NORTH-EAST CONNECTION?

At least four of the twelve *mohelim* in Joseph Blank's list had connections with the North-East. Claff, Applebaum and Yelin had been, successively, readers of the Newcastle synagogue. Reverend Ostroff had some association with Newcastle, where he is recorded as having addressed a Zionist meeting in 1901 (*JC*, 4th January 1901, p.22). Among the London Association of Mohelim, four out of seven *mohelim* were connected with the North-East. These were Applebaum, Yelin, Ostroff and Tertis. The last-named is described in Olsover (op. cit., p.303) as a former minister of the Jewish congregation in West Hartlepool.

ILLUSTRATIONS

A. David Applebaum in canonicals, portrait probably taken while he was reader of the Newcastle synagogue (1886-94)

B. David Applebaum in canonicals, portrait probably taken a year or two before his death in 1907

C. Dobrin (Dobrzyn)
Synagogue, interior

D. Dobrin (Dobrzyn)
Synagogue, exterior

Dobrzyn n. Wisłą   Ilica Franciszańska

E. Dobrin (Dobrzyn) – Jewish shops , Franciszanska Street

Illustrations C, D and E by courtesy of Julian Preisler,
www.jpreisler.com/dobrzyn

F. Jeanette Applebaum,
taken in about 1925

G. Jeanette Applebaum,
taken at the seaside,
probably Cliftonville,
sometime in the 1930s

H. Inscription at base of David Applebaum's gravestone: " MEMBER OF THE SONS OF DOBRIN & HEBREW ORDER OF DRUIDS". Jewish gravestones in England at this time often bore the name of the friendly societies that paid for them

I. David Applebaum's gravestone at Plashet cemetery, East Ham, London (G18 No 26)

J. Synagogue, Leazes Park Road,
Newcastle upon Tyne.
Photographer, Bob Skingle, 2002
© English Heritage

Unless otherwise stated, the words or phrases below are in Hebrew and have been transliterated into Ashkenazi pronunciation, as David Applebaum and his family would have used, rather than the Sephardi pronunciation in which Modern Hebrew is spoken.

Ashkenazi - relating to Jews from Germany and Eastern Europe.

Baal Korah – skilled Torah reader.

Barmitzvah – age of majority of a boy at 13 years

Beth Din – a Jewish religious court.

Bris (short for *Bris Millah*) – circumcision

Chassidim – followers of a mystical and fervently pious Jewish religious movement originating in Eastern Europe in the eighteenth century.

Chazan (plural, *chazanim*) – synagogue cantor; in Britain a "reader".

Cheder – religious school

Chevra or *chevrah* (plural, *chevrot*) – a society or club for religious purposes; a small synagogue.

Chevrah Torah – society for the study of the Torah.

Dayan – religious judge; member of a *beth din*.

Gemara – the body of text which grew up as a commentary and supplement to oral Jewish law; part of the *Talmud*.

Landsmanshaft (plural - *Landsmanshaftn*) (Yiddish) – a Jewish benefit society of immigrants from the same town.

Maggid – a traditional Jewish preacher, often itinerant and not connected with any individual synagogue.

Mikvah – ritual bath.

Minyan – quorum of ten males of thirteen and above required for a full service.

Mohel – ritual circumciser.

Rosh Hashonah – the Jewish New Year.

Sephardi – relating to Jews from Spain and Portugal.

Shabbos – Sabbath day.

Shochet – ritual slaughterer.

Shtetl (Yiddish) – small Jewish town.

Shul (Yiddish) - a synagogue.

Succos – Feast of Tabernacles.

Talmud – the classic collection of rabbinic law and commentary, which includes the *Gemara*, recording legal decisions and discussions, some over two thousand years old.

Torah – the Pentateuch; the first five books of the Old Testament.

Trefah – not kosher.

Yom Kippur – Day of Atonement.